MEDIEVAL VISIONS
OF HEAVEN AND HELL

GARLAND MEDIEVAL BIBLIOGRAPHIES
(VOL. 11)

GARLAND REFERENCE LIBRARY
OF THE HUMANITIES
(VOL. 1256)

GARLAND MEDIEVAL BIBLIOGRAPHIES

MEDIEVAL VISIONS OF HEAVEN AND HELL

A *Sourcebook*

Eileen Gardiner

Routledge
Taylor & Francis Group

LONDON AND NEW YORK

1993

First published 1993 by Garland Publishing, Inc.

Published 2018 by Routledge
2 Park Square, Milton Park, Abingdon, Oxon OX14 4RN
605 Third Avenue, New York, NY 10017

First issued in paperback 2021

Routledge is an imprint of the Taylor & Francis Group, an informa business

Library of Congress Cataloging-in-Publication Data

Gardiner, Eileen.
    Medieval visions of heaven and hell : a sourcebook / by Eileen
Gardiner.
        p.   cm. — (Garland medieval bibliographies ; vol. 11)
(Garland reference library of the humanities ; vol. 1256)
    Includes bibliographical references and index.
    ISBN 0–8240–3348–5 (alk. paper)
    1. Visions—Bibliography. 2. Heaven—Christianity—Bibliography.
3. Hell—Christianity—Bibliography.   I. Title. II. Series. III. Series:
Garland reference library of the humanities ; vol. 1256.
Z7794.G37   1993
[BT833]
016.2482'9—dc20   92–45794
                                                                      CIP

ISBN 13: 978-1-03-210009-8 (pbk)
ISBN 13: 978-0-8240-3348-4 (hbk)

To my mother
and
to the memory of my father

CONTENTS

PREFACE

During my work on this project I have been surprised by the number of new works to be added to the list of visions. Some have been added through the work of scholars investigating woman saints and mystics,[1] some through closer examination and clearer identification of texts included in chronicles and letters. When Fritzsche[2] published his list of visions in 1886–87, he included thirty-two, but almost one-third of these were not visions of heaven and hell. Many of the visions that have often been included in standard lists and assumed to be visions of heaven and hell, such as the *Vision of Raduin,* are, in fact, not. They may be visions of a particular saint or a visitation by a devil, but they do not deal with the geography, either physical or spiritual, of the otherworld. Without doubt, my list will soon be found to be incomplete, but it was only this realization that enabled me to publish what I had uncovered so far, secure in the knowledge that my patient publisher and interested scholars would prefer a volume before this century closed.

The first wave of research on the subject of visions of heaven and hell was in the late nineteenth century. Many of the first editions were prepared at that time in England, Italy and Germany. We seem to be in a new period of interest in

1. Elizabeth Alvilda Petroff, *Medieval Women's Visionary Literature* (New York: Oxford, 1986); Jo Ann McNamara, and John E. Halborg. *Sainted Women of the Dark Ages* (Durham, N.C. and London: Duke University Press, 1992).
2. Fritzsche, C. "Die lateinischen Visionen des Mittelalters bis zur Mitte des 12. Jahrhunderts." *Romanische Forschungen* 2 (1886): 247–79; 3 (1887): 337–69.

this field with important works appearing annually in Europe and the United States. Historical and religious studies remain important, while psychological and the new critical methodology have also be applied to these texts.

The following bibliography includes all the identified Christian visions of heaven and hell from Western Europe during the Middle Ages, with the exception of the *Divine Comedy*, which would require several volumes of this length to even begin to examine the scholarly work in English. It includes visions in all European languages. It covers the literature on these works since 1850, although occasionally earlier works might be included. It is generally limited to works in the major European languages, although some exceptions have been made when there is a significant body of recent work in one of the less-frequently cited languages, for instance the recent work in the Netherlands on the *Voyage of St. Brendan.* In general, dissertations have not been included, and *Dissertations Abstracts International* should be consulted independently.

There are two parts to this volume. The first part is devoted to general material on vision literature and includes works that are broad in scope, often covering visions from a general perspective or a particular point of view, such as political or apocalyptic. These general works should be consulted whenever a particular work is investigated, because they may include extensive discussions of particular visions, but often in such a cursory fashion that it was impossible to cross-reference them. When the discussion was more particular these works have been cross-referenced. The second part of this book is divided into fifty-three chapters by vision. These chapters are arranged alphabetically by the name of the visionary, except in the cases of St. Patrick's Purgatory, where the various medieval visions associated with that location are included under the name of the pilgrimage site; and both St. Gregory the Great and Otloh of Emmeran, where the visions are included under the title of the book in which they were found. A total of sixty-two visions are covered.

Each of these vision chapters is divided into two sections. The first is an introduction to the text, giving its historical background, language, a brief synopsis, and mention of any significant details about the vision in comparison to other texts. The second section is the bibliography for the work. It is divided into two parts, the first including the editions and translations of the work and the second including studies on the work. Each entry is annotated. The bibliography section may begin with a listing of bibliographies if the work has been treated recently by a significant bibliographical study.

A brief list of abbreviations is included, as well as indexes by author and subject.

The research for this volume was carried out primarily at the New York Public Research Library, and I sincerely thank the librarians and staff there, and particularly the Cooperative Services librarians who made it possible for me to obtain access to material not in the NYPL collection. Additional research was carried out at the libraries of Columbia University and Fordham University, and I thank those institutions and their librarians for their assistance.

And always, my thanks to Ron Musto, who never failed with the encouragement and enthusiasm of a true friend.

INTRODUCTION

The present volume covers the currently identified Christian visions of heaven and hell (excluding Dante's *Divine Comedy*) from western Europe during the Middle Ages from the late sixth through the fourteenth century. These literary works purport to describe actual visions of the realm entered by souls after death. These visions were an extraordinarily popular literary genre in the Middle Ages. More than sixty are now known to have survived, many of these in multiple manuscripts and many with versions in several languages. They are found in the chronicles of the period and in the manuscript books bound together with various works from doctrinal treatises to romances. Their influence is apparent in both religious and popular literature throughout this period, such as sermons and romances, and in the alliterative dream visions of later generations of writers.[1]

THE IDEA OF VISION

The term "vision" is clearly in itself problematical, but the problem with this word has often been noted. One major reason for the problem is that in English there might not exist an appropriate word. We have only two words; "dream" and "vision" – the former obviously connected with sleep, but the later left to deal with all other non-natural visual experiences.

As Carolly Erickson notes: "In his commentary on the Somnium Scipionis Macrobius defined five categories of dreams" not of dreams and visions, but just of dreams:

somnium	enigmatic dream
visio	prophetic dream
oraculum	oracular dream
insomnium	nightmare
visum	apparition

The last two originate in the mind of the dreamer. In an oracular dream, a venerable or religious man (or a god) reveals what is to come and advises the dreamer about how to prepare himself for it. Prophetic visions are glimpses of the future itself, while in enigmatic dreams a particular message is conveyed though "concealed with strange shapes and veiled with ambiguity."[2]

In *De Genesi ad litteram,* Augustine delineated three types of visions: corporeal vision (*visio corporealis*), seeing the incorporeal through natural optical perception; spiritual or imaginative vision (*visio spiritualis* or *imaginativa*), seeing incorporeal shapes, as in dreaming; and intellectual vision (*visio intellectualis*), direct sight of incorporeal beings and imageless concepts.[3] Dinzelbacher in 1981[4] writes of visions, apparitions, dream visions and dream apparitions, ecstasies, and mysticism.

Obviously those seeking to describe these experiences, from one end of the spectrum to the other, have been faced with the problem of defining something, even though they are not quite sure of the nature of the thing itself. It is, however, clear that they are attempting to describe extraordinary events during which they experience, through the senses, the physical reality of the world that we call the "otherworld," the world beyond death – the Christian otherworld of heaven, hell, and purgatory.

The visions collected here significantly reflect the popular and clerical views of the nature of the realm of this otherworld. This realm first included the regions of heaven and hell. Hell was often described as a region of purgatorial punishment through which sinners would progress in the hope of complete purgation before the coming of the Last Judgment. These two regions were later expanded to include purgatory, which served the same function as the purgatorial hell. Our contemporary view of the Christian otherworld leads us to distinguish these three places, the medieval view, even before the introduction of purgatory, was somewhat more complicated. It included various stages of paradise, segregated according to degree of the inhabitants' holiness, culminating at the throne of the Lord, a view seldom granted to visionaries from the realm of the living. Hell was a series of descents ending at the pit of hell where the devil himself dwelt. Between these two extremes was a wide range of tortures and a more limited range of pleasures. And this range was extended even further when purgatory was officially introduced into the otherworld in the twelfth century.[5]

Those who recorded these visions, the redactors, with the possible exception of Marcus, the redactor of the *Vision of Tundale*, seldom gave great care to specifically segmenting the otherworld. The complexity of this otherworld is evident from the *Divine Comedy*, which was the most highly developed medieval vision of heaven and hell. Here are nine circles of hell, with heaven beginning at the earthly paradise and continuing through its nine spheres to the empyrean, to which might then be added the twelve stages of ante-purgatory and purgatory. Thus when our visionary speaks of heaven, hell, or purgatory, we cannot limit our minds to fixed locations, easily definable and unambiguous.

APOCALYPTIC AND MYSTICAL VISIONS

Considering the complexity of the medieval otherworld, some readers will readily assume that other types of visions are included in the following material, and most surely will assume that dream visions, mystical visions, and apocalyptic visions are included under this rubric. This work, however, is limited to visions of heaven, hell, and purgatory.

The earliest Christian visions of the otherworlds were actually apocalyptic. The visions of Peter, Paul and Mary, visions of the last judgment, were extremely influential on later visions, which were, however, less concerned with the end-time than with the co-existent otherworld – the place where the recently dead might be found.

Bernard McGinn explains the distinction between apocalypses and visions:

> Visions share some of the characteristics of the classical apocalypses; such as intermediary revealing figures, interest in the heavenly realities, and stress upon coming judgment; but looked at as a whole, it is obvious that they form a genre of their own.... visionary literature [is] increasingly centered on the fate of the individual soul; on the other [hand, apocalyptic visions include] a variety of texts linked by more general historical concerns, especially a view of the present as a moment of supreme crisis [that] frequently, though not invariably, incorporate concern with the structure of history, usually in terms of a theory of world ages.[6]

Of the visions included here, only the *Vision of St. Paul,* which has roots in early Christian literature but remained vital throughout the entire Middle Ages, is an apocalyptic vision.

The mystical vision also forms a separate genre. The experience of these visionaries, although sometimes characterized by certain similarities, is, in essence, different from that of otherworld visionaries. Mystical experiences often are preserved in a totally different form of writing. They are found in the journals, biographies, or confessional writings of the mystic or, as was often the case with women not fully educated to literacy, in the writings of their confessors. These works recount the personal struggle of the soul toward union with the divine and appear in the context of a life devoted to the mystical ascent.

However, most visions of heaven and hell come to us in a very different guise. They are generally isolated events in the life of the visionary, although that life might be dramatically altered by the vision. They are often separate works of literature, preserved as independent pieces, and found in manuscripts with hagiography and romance. In other cases these visions are included in the chronicles and associated with specific dates, reflecting their importance as historical events for the community. In Bede's *Historia ecclesiastica,* for example, we find the *Vision of Furseus,* the *Vision of Drythelm,* and the *Vision of the Monk of Bernicia.* The *Vision of Walkelin* appears in the *Chronicle of Odericus Vitalus.* Many are repeated in Roger of Wendover's *Chronicle,* and many more in Vincent of Beauvais' *Speculum historiale.* However, their importance as events in the history of a community should not be confused with the essentially historical nature of apocalyptic literature. Here the judgment, the essential element of apocalyptic literature, indicates the culmination of history and the focal point of all human endeavor. Visions of heaven and hell are not necessarily books that define the ages of history, nor are they manifestations of the struggle of the individual toward the deified life, as Underhill described the life of the mystic.

As mentioned above, the Vision of Paul fits into two categories: apocalyptic visions and otherworld visions. There is also a certain crossover between mystical and otherworld visionaries, which can be recognized in four visions included here: the visions of Monk of Eynsham, of Marguerite D'Oingt, of Christina Mirabilis, and of St. Sadalburga. The first is clearly within the genre of visions of heaven and hell, but some elements of the vision correspond to elements of mystical vision literature, since in his vision of the glorified Christ, the monk seems to transcend himself and approaches a uniative experience that could be classified as mystical. Since this monk has never been named, identifying him as a mystic is impossible. The distinction is, of course, that mystics have mystical visions, but the visions of other visionaries cannot be called mystical visions.

The latter three mentioned, Marguerite D'Oingt, Christina Mirabilis, and St. Sadalburga, are visionaries and mystics; and among their mystical experiences and visions they received a glimpse of the otherworld. Both Elizabeth of Schönau[7] (1129–65) and Hildegard of Bingen[8] (1098–1179) were also mystics who experienced numerous visions. Among these were glimpses of the otherworld, but within the content of their extraordinarily visionary life, it seems difficult to isolate otherworld visions from the rest and to make them in any way definitive of the religious lives of these two women.

One particular characteristic to distinguish mystical from otherworld visions is that they are not location-specific; mystical visions involve the transformation of the soul and not, in general, the knowledge of something external to the soul. They are often the result of long practice and devotion.

However, in commenting on mystical visions, Evelyn Underhill, reflecting the caution of her subjects regarding these experiences, writes: "'Vision,' that vaguest of words, has been used by friends and enemies of the mystics to describe or obscure a wide range of experience: from formless intuition, through crude optical hallucination, to the voluntary visualizations common to the artistic mind."[9]

As noted above, although there are some instances where the two types of visionary experience might overlap, the vision of heaven and hell is not necessarily a mystical vision, even though a mystical vision might include a vision of heaven and/or hell. When we speak of mystical visions we are speaking of them as coming from a specific group of individuals who have followed the course of perfection. Their visions are somehow, although not always positively, connected with this struggle for perfection. However, visions of heaven and hell are often the result of happenstance and illness. Otherworld visionaries can be saint or sinners, kings or peasants, but the validity of otherworld visions is not bound by the fact that they may have been induced by fasting, hardship, or disease.

Although Tundale was a sinner, struck by his vision in the midst of a wicked deed, Carolly Erickson notes that

"What Tundale saw was nothing less than a visual distillation of ultimate truth, played out in a dimension outside time. Yet this distillation was not, in fact, independent either of time or of earthly affairs. It was intimately linked to the chain of human lifetimes....The events of hell and purgatory were the final sum of all earthly sin; those of paradise the essence of all earthly virtue. No corner of history was omitted from this overarching logic; judged against it, the present took on new meanings."[10]

Dream visions, which are also excluded from this study form a group which, in reality, have nothing to do with either dreams of visions but are frames for medieval allegorical works in which the author poses as a dreamer in a highly self-conscious work to expound on a subject through the convenient device of a dream where the constraints of reality do not apply.[11]

VISIONS AND VOYAGES

So many of these visions are like voyages to the otherworld, since the visionary usually seems to be physically present. It is, therefore, important to consider the notion of voyage as opposed to the notion of vision.

The word "vision" is generally used to designate the type of work considered here, but, in fact, "vision," which the OED defines as "an appearance of a prophetic or mystical character, or having the nature of a revelation supernaturally presented to the mind either in sleep or in an abnormal state," may not always be completely appropriate and may even be contrary to the spirit of works like *St. Brendan's Voyage* and the texts associated with St. Patrick's Purgatory.

In these cases "voyage" would undeniably be a more suitable word. It certainly best describes what happens in *St. Brendan's Voyage,* where there is no separation of the soul from the body. Brendan's body and soul together actually get into a boat with seventeen of his companions and set sail in search of the Land of Promise of the Saints. They travel to hell and back. These places are not found in a trance or dream or in some superconscious state, but, presumably, in the waters of the Atlantic.

St. Brendan's Voyage actually belongs to the genre of the *imrama*, the Irish sea-voyage narrative. The *imrama* usually describe pilgrimages undertaken to seek God; there is an overtly religious aspect to the voyage. Visions of heaven and hell and *imrama* are, in general, distinct groups, but in the case of *St. Brendan's Voyage,* the two genres overlap. This particular *imrama* had a significant impact on otherworld literature and deserves to be considered in this context, especially since it is particularly Christian, whereas many of its antecedents have ancient pagan associations. But I have not included other *imrama,* even though an important one, the *Voyage of the Húi Corra,* which significantly influenced the *Voyage of Brendan,* includes both a vision of heaven and hell and the idea of voyage as pilgrimage. I have let Brendan, a Christian *imrama,* stand as representative of this related pagan genre, which merits treatment in an entirely separate volume.

The overlapping of the function of vision and pilgrimage, as glimpsed in the *imrama,* is important also when considering the texts associated with the western Irish pilgrimage site, St. Patrick's Purgatory. From the original *Tractatus* to later works, such as the *Vision of William Staunton,* this pilgrimage destination, unlike most other pilgrimage sites, was a vehicle for visions of the otherworld, but the lines between vision and voyage again become blurred, as with *St. Brendan's Voyage.*

Voyage literature, hagiography, utopian literature, history, and biography are all related to this genre, because the idea of vision, if not the fact of vision, is implicit in the literary process. However, voyage literature is related to vision literature on another level. Besides its function of revealing the unknown, throughout this period voyage literature identified the "other" not in the otherworld, but in this world across the known borders, just as vision literature identified the "other" in the regions of hell among the devils and other infernal creatures. Mary Campbell notes how medieval perceptions of the other as evil, "images of both self and other...have some explanatory value when we consider the catastrophical historical climax of premodern European contact with the outside." This dark other that voyage literature portrays is the direct descendent of the dark other that inhabits the infernal regions of hell. The *Vision of Tundale* and Mandeville's *Travels* are close cousins, both of them projecting our fears onto an evil other.

Though they may be related on some psychological level, voyage and vision literature are two distinct genres; and "voyage" has particular and specific definitions. What can be said in support of the word "vision" is that in all cases we are dealing primarily with a visual experience, although in these works a great emphasis is also connected with the visionary's experience of the otherworld through other senses, such as smell, hearing, and even taste. But even more importantly, these otherworld visions are often presented as total physical experiences, since a visionary might suffer pain and bring back scars of torture from these "visions." Furseus and Tundale both suffer actual physical punishment. The Knight Owein in St. Patrick's Purgatory also suffers a great deal, but unlike Tundale and Furseus whose souls and bodies are separated for this experience, Owein enters the Purgatory with body and soul together; and there is no indication that the visionary Walkelin, who also bears the scars of his ordeal, endures any separation of body and soul.

VISIONS OF HEAVEN AND HELL

Many medieval visions of the otherworld focused often on the punishment of the damned – usually witnessed by a saintly visionary. These might be called "justice-seeking" visions of the otherworld since they revealed a place where justice was meted out, reflecting strongly the judgmental tone of the earlier apocalyptic visions mentioned above. Visions like the *Vision of Adamnán* and the visions from Gregory the Great's *Dialogues* fall into this category.

Another type of vision, which was particularly popular, might be called as "penance-producing visions." These featured hell and purgatory as instructional devices to warn the visionary to return to earth and do good or to return to earth and undertake masses, prayers, and penance for those already dead. The visions might also keep the living in line as they paid the clergy to help the dead. The visions of Tundale and Drythelm are examples of this type. There were also some visions in this category that took on the aspect of "political" visions, in that the visionary viewed the formerly-powerful of the earth, including kings and popes, subject to punishments in the otherworld, and brought back tidings of their suffering, which might serve as warning to those currently in power. The *Vision of Charles the Fat* and the *Vision of Bernoldus* are probably the best examples of this type.

Let us now look at what we have in this literature that has reached us; what these written documents actually are. These works, which we call visions of heaven and hell, are not exactly reports of the visions themselves. In fact, they are, in most cases, literary productions, often several times removed from the actual accounts of the returning visionary.

Once the visionary is no longer "raptus ab humanis rebus" he or she describes the experience. In some cases it is recorded that an immediate acquaintance of the visionary, such as the cleric in the *Vision of Gottschalk,* wrote down the visionary's description, but often the record left to us is found in a chronicle, after it has become the hearsay of an age. In effect, it is most likely that although there may be some correlation between the experience of the visionary and the piece of literature, the experience has been converted to literature through the operation of two factors: one involving the verbal skills of the visionary and the other reflecting the forces operating on the visionary's amanuensis or redactor.

Our problem of "textuality" is thus many-layered, since there are many stages of authorship and text between the vision experience and the final literary work. First, even granting the objective reality of the vision experience, we must confront the problem of the visionary attempting to articulate an experience of the ineffable. The visionary's mind relied on the tool of language to express the visionary experience, and language is a limited tool for quantifying and qualifying experiences. So the visionary in relying on the tools available, will find them to be somewhat inadequate. Also he or she will rely on the tools others have used to describe similar experiences, and therefore, the visions will take on a sameness in articulation. It should be noted that mystics like Marguerite D'Oingt, who may have felt free to use a more poetic and, therefore, more richly impressionistic vocabulary, often stun the reader by the images they are able to elicit. However, in general, there is a stylistic consistency over the range of vision literature that, on one level, may stem largely from the limited verbal tools of the visionary.

Once the story has passed from the visionary to the amanuensis, we can expect two forces at work leveling any literary radicalism in the text of the vision. Primarily we have the operation of homogeneity, which follows the tendency to make things increasingly easy to understand. What seems incomprehensible is traditionally made readily accessible by an amanuensis or a scribe; often they change the sense of the original to conform to a sense of what is normal. When dealing with a literature of the supernatural, there is a constant effort to make the supernatural more manageable.

The other operation on the text, and one that is difficult to trace and impossible to prove, but nevertheless must be considered, is the process of making a text conform to prevailing viewpoints. In the period we are discussing we must consider the influence of a powerful political institution, the Church, as well as the political power of smaller institutions, such as the religious orders and the local bishops. We might cast this process in the malicious light of a particularly evil institution attempting to control the populace, as did many scholars of the late nineteenth and early twentieth centuries, or we might recognize it as the natural inclination of all institutions. But we, nevertheless, must consider it part of the very nature of the Church to attempt to enclose, contain, and define all manifestations of popular piety. What remains then is not the record of the vision of an individual, but an account filtered by minds that have not had a visionary experience

Underhill wrote:

> Since no one can know what it is really like to have a vision, but the visionaries themselves,...it is as impossible for those who have never heard a voice or seen a vision to discuss these experiences with intelligence, as it is for stay-at-homes to discuss the passions of the battle-field on the material supplied by war correspondents. No second-hand account can truly report the experience of the person whose perceptions or illusions present themselves in this form.[12]

HEAVEN, HELL, AND PURGATORY

Once we recognize what these documents called "visions" of heaven and hell are, we can recognize that they reveal not the vision itself but the popular medieval Christian view of heaven and hell expressed in an ambitiously graphic style.

Heaven and hell, as expressed in these visions, is not actually a description of what the visionary saw, but a literary interpretation of what the visionary said that he or she saw. And here the function of fantasy is operating at full force, especially when challenged to describe evil. There is almost no limit to confabulating more and more diverse tortures to warn about the place to which the evil life leads. Unfortunately this power of imagination to evil probably is fueled by and fuels reality, and the accounts of the martyrdoms of the early Christian saints vie with the imaginations of authors for gruesome detail and unthinkable torment.

Punishment in hell almost universally involves fire. Often cold is added, and souls are tossed back and forth from one to the other. Pitchforks and other sharp implements are popular among the demons for moving the crowds of souls through the infernal regions. Awful smells and horrendous noise are associated with hell, along with other assaults on the tactile and visual senses. Hell is clearly imagined and described over and over. Often the details are the same – fire, bridges, burning lakes, horrid little creatures pulling out sinners' entrails. They are physical, colorful, vivid images. They are very often related to the masculine images of work provided by the nascent industrial economy. Forges, furnaces, hammers, smoke, and burning metals combine to present a picture that would certainly be hellish to a rural, aristocratic, or agrarian audience. An excellent example occurs in the "Volcanic Island" episode of the *Voyage of St. Brendan*. The demons usually inflict torments from the outside, but there are also vipers in many of the visions that infest the "bodies" of the souls and torture them by consuming their bones and flesh. Many of these punishments are also found in purgatory, once it becomes part of the otherworld, or in the purgative regions found in many visions before purgatory became a doctrine of the church.

By contrast, heaven is a pale place, basically without any reality. Any student of literature has been confronted by the difficulty of the heroic Satan of Milton's *Paradise Lost* and the weakness of God and heaven when described in opposition to hell. Is this a problem that is innate to the heavenly? Did heaven have a reality for the visionary? Was it ineffable, unable to be described, and thus beyond the imagination of the writer to express? There is the lure of the devil as other. But, God, as the hidden (within) that we prefer not to explore or that perhaps can be found when we search for the other, and the heaven God inhabits, seem beyond the limits of the imagination.

Heaven is always glowing and white, bright – often so bright that one cannot see for the brightness. There are many people; and there is a focal point of brightness. There are often beautiful clothes and gems, perhaps high walls and flowery fields. Heaven has a fragrant smell, more light, less noise, and perhaps even sweet music.

Descriptions of heaven often include both ideal urban and natural elements. The later are derived from descriptions of places like the Elysian Fields and are characterized by an abundance of trees, flowers, and fruit. Often these scenes included the brightly colored pavilions. The urban details are tied to both the developing urban sensibility in medieval Europe and an understanding of the Heavenly Jerusalem from the *Apocalypse*. Yet the urban descriptions, though a highly developed medieval genre, are somewhat limited in these visions, as if their authors were not sure about what constituted an ideal city, and perhaps their audiences were really more likely to associate a real city with hell. These urban descriptions, however, always include beautiful walls, constructed of bright and precious materials. They might seem like gold and, like the Heavenly Jerusalem, are often full of gems and precious stones. There are buildings, often described as halls without walls, so that one can enter from all sides. The idea of entry seems important in these fanciful urban descriptions, because just as the halls or houses have no doors, which might be closed, the walls often have no gates, and the visionary is miraculously transported to the other side of every wall.

Perhaps these descriptions reflect the ideal of the noble life more accurately than of urban fabric. But finally it seems that heaven is not "other." The descriptions of it reflected the reality of the noble life, which, if not seen, was described in the romances and chronicles. If we attempt to articulate a modern understanding of the nature of the heavenly, it would probably be best described as unity – psychic, physical, spiritual. But a description of heaven or unity is again limited by language. The very nature of words is much better suited to hell – heaven is best revealed or described not in words but perhaps in a mandala – some visual unity. This is extremely difficult to elaborate verbally. The feeling of unity and wholeness is much more profoundly difficult to describe than diversity since language is fundamentally rich in that it is diverse, and unity is ineffable.

Peter Dronke explains that "...in the mystical Platonic tradition that Dionysius has transmitted to the medieval

West, the unfitting and the monstrous is, by its sheer bafflement of human attempts to imagine the divine, most apt to convey truly how far the divine is beyond all imaginings."[13] In other words, with the premise that the *bonum perfectum* is the unknowable and therefore indescribable, attention turns to the *malum perfectum* for its reflective values in understanding the ineffable.

Another reason heaven is difficult to write about is that it is essentially egalitarian – that is, ideally all people in heaven are together unless a structure is imposed, as in the Divine Comedy where Dante used Plato's Timeas as a model. In pleasure or joy, there is not division but wholeness – integrity.

UTOPIAN OR MYTHIC PROJECTIONS

Visions of heaven and hell combine the dystopian and utopian projections of the medieval mind. As Louis Mumford explained regarding the latter: "the utopia of the first fifteen hundred years after Christ is transplanted to the sky, and called the Kingdom of Heaven."[14] It is the same process confronting authors and social planners who try to conjure up a picture of an ideal society. Usually we think of utopian literature in terms of the technological elements that have pervaded modern examples of this genre, citing these improvements as desired goals. It is often a society of material betterment – a highly organized society, where people cooperate and sublimate their own individual desires to the good of the whole, but in a strictly material context. They have, however, nothing to do with real perfectibility – the wholeness which is attainable, not outside, but within. Vision literature often projects the idea of the perfectibility of the human condition. In this sense, therefore, vision literature is utopian. There is some striving in the descriptions of heaven to project a vision of unity and wholeness, which would accord even with contemporary notions of salvation.

It is also important to consider the relationship of this literature to the realm of the mythic which has been critically explored since the late nineteenth century beginning with Sir James Frazer, most notably in The Golden Bough, and through the twentieth century by such important figures as Marcea Eliade, Joseph Campbell, Carlo Ginzburg, and James Hillman, who examine the role played by the other-world and the passage back and forth from this to the other in shamanistic rites, dreams, and rituals.

There are many features of the witches' sabbath noted in Ginzburg's *Ecstasies,* for example, that reflect the content of the visions of the otherworld: the traveller lies as if dead while journeying to the land of the dead; the returning traveller brings back news of, and requests from, the dead; the traveller often engages in combat with those met in the otherworld. There are two additional, occasional similarities: the soul leaving the body may be described as a little bird or butterfly; and the time of the visions may correspond to the usual time of the witches' sabbath – at the end of the year or the first days of January, often referred to as ember days. The nocturnal assembly described in the *Vision of Walkelin* and elements of the *Vision of Olav Aesteson* clearly reflect the rites of the witches' sabbaths as described in the documents presented by Ginzburg.

Campbell speaks of this urge toward contact with the realm of the otherworld as an attempt to reassure humanity confronted with its existential condition,

> and the answer found [is] one that has been giving comfort to those who wish comfort ever since,

namely: "Nothing dies; death and birth are but a threshold crossing, back and forth, as it were, through a veil."[15]...With an identified center in central Europe dating from the third interglacial period and a range extending, on the one hand, eastward to Labrador and, on the other, southward to Rhodesia, an abundantly documented mythology of the hunt has flourished....The main idea would seem to be that there is no such thing as death, but simply...a passing back and forth of an immortal individual through a veil."[16]

Although similarities are apparent, there is nothing conclusive to relate visions of heaven and hell to these other rituals, but given the developing nature of this field it would be rash to assume that correspondences might not be found when suitably investigated. Ginzburg himself found it difficult to tie all the strands of his thesis together in a conventional way; but he could not escape the urge to compare the remarkable similarities that he identified and attempt to make sense of the impulse toward the otherworld.

NOTES

1. A. C. Spearing, *Medieval Dream-Poetry* (Cambridge: Cambridge University Press, 1976), pp. 11–16.

2. Carolly Erickson, *The Medieval Vision* (New York: Oxford University Press, 1976), pp. 36–37.

3. Ibid, p. 37.

4. Peter Dinzelbacher, *Vision und Visionsliteratur im Mittelalters* (Stuttgart: Hiersemann, 1981) pp. 29–56.

5. Jacques Le Goff, *The Birth of Purgatory* (Chicago: University of Chicago Press, 1984), pp. 130–32.

6. Bernard McGinn, *Visions of the End: Apocalyptic Traditions in the Middle Ages* (New York: Columbia University Press, 1979), p. 15

7. "Sanctae Elisabeth Vita," PL 195:119–9; Elizabeth Alvilda Petroff, *Medieval Women's Visionary Literature* (New York: Oxford University Press, 1986), pp. 159–70.

8. "Hildegardis Scivias," *Corpus Christianorum continuatio medievalis* 3 (Turnholt: Brepols, 1978); Hildegard of Bingen, *Scivias* (Sante Fe, N.M.: Bear & Co., 1986); Francesca Maria Steele, *The Life and Visions of St. Hildegarde* (London: Heath, Cranston, and Ousely, 1941); Prudentia Brath, M. Immaculata Ritscher, and Joseph Schmidt Gorg, *Hildegarden von Bingen Leider* (Salzburg: Otto Muller, 1969); Hildegard of Bingen, *Scivias,* trans. by Columba Hart and Jane Bishop (New York: Paulist Press, 1990).

9. Evelyn Underhill, *Mysticism* (New York: Dutton, 1961), p. 279.

10. Erickson, p. 217.

11. Spearing, pp. 2–4.

12. Underhill, p. 279.

13. Peter Dronke, *Dante and Medieval Latin Traditions* (Cambridge: Cambridge Univbersity Press, 1986), p. 24.

14. Louis Mumford, *The Story of Utopias* (New York: Viking, 1962), p. 59.

15. Joseph Campbell, *Primitive Mythology* (New York: Penguin, 1976), p. 342

16. Ibid, p. 348.

ABBREVIATIONS

AB   Analecta Bollandiana (Brussels: Société des Bollandistes, 1882–).

AS   Acta Sanctorum...*editio novissima*. Ed. J. Carnandet et al. Paris: Palmé, 1863–).

BHL   *Bibliotheca hagiographica* latinae *antiquae et mediae aetatis*. Brussels: Socii Bollandiani, 1898–).

MGH   Monumenta Germaniae historica. Scriptores rerum Germanicrum and Scriptores... nova ser. (Hannover: Gesellschaft für ältere deutsche Geschishtskunde, 1826–).

MGH PLAC   Monumenta Germania Historia, *Poetae latini aevi Carolini*. (Hannover: Gesellschaft für ältere deutsche Geschishtskunde, 1880–1951).

MGH SRM   Monumenta Germania Historia, Scriptores rerum merovingicarum. (Hannover: Gesellschaft für ältere deutsche Geschishtskunde, 1884–1920).

PL   Patrologiae cursus completus. Series Latina. Ed. by J.–P. Migne. (Paris: Migne, 1844–65).

GENERAL STUDIES ON VISION LITERATURE

1   Alexander, Paul J. "Medieval Apocalypses as Historical Sources." *American Historical Review* 73 (1968): 997–1018.

Discusses the rich historical information that might be found in medieval apocalypses, and although it does not discuss visions particularly, it provides an insight into the material that can be found in these works.

2   Amat, Jacqueline. *Songes et visions: L'au-delà dans la littérature latine tardive.* Paris: Études Augustiniennes, 1985.

Examines texts from the second to sixth century in an attempt to concretely retrace the mentality of the time in relation to the afterlife and how this is shown in the literature (songs and visions) especially in the images used to describe the afterlife. Deals with the literary sources as well as the collective imagination of the time. Jungian-influenced approach.

3   Ancona, Alessandro D'. *I precursori di Dante.* Florence: G. Sansoni, 1874.

Treats the antecedents of Dante in general and gives some particular attention to the Paul, Brendan, Tundale, Patrick and Alberic visions. He does not make firm connections between these and the *Divine Comedy,* but indicates a general millieu of vision literature, which does not detract from Dante's originality.

4   Aubrun, Michel. "Caractères et portée religieuse et sociales des 'Visiones' en Occident du vi^e au xie siecle." *Cahiers de Civilisation Médiévale* 23 (1980): 109–30.

Discusses the position of the visionary and the redactor with regard to ecclesiastical authority and marginality.

5   Bar, F. *Les routes de l'autre monde: Descentes aux enfers et voyages dans l'au delà.* Paris: Presses Universitaires de France, 1946.

Various chapters include discussions of the works under consideration here. *St. Patrick's Purgatory* is discussed with *imrama* in a chapter in Celtic literature; in one on medieval literature there is discussion of Gregory the Great, Wetti, Drythelm, Alberic, and Tundale, as well as a discussion of the relationship among voyages to the earthly paradise, romances, and allegories. There are chapters on Dante and post-Dantean texts, and an appendix on paradise. Concludes that there is a great diversity in this literature, and that as religious texts they were designed to edify and instruct through the revelation of those victorious in heaven and those punished in hell.

6   Becker, Ernest J. *A Contribution to the Comparative Study of the Medieval Visions of Heaven and Hell.* Baltimore: J. Murphy, 1899.

A seminal book in the study of visions of heaven and hell. Part I discusses the various sources for medieval visions in earlier cultures and the development of vision literature. Parts II and III concentrate on Anglo-Saxon and Middle English visions, respectively.

7   Benz, Ernst. *Die Vision: Erfahrungsformen und Bilderwelt.* Stuttgart: Ernst Klett, 1969.

Broad study including the relationship of visions to disease and training, the role of the visionary and his or her experience, the tradition of visions and the religious worldview of visionaries.

8   ———. "Vision und Führung in der christlichen Mystik." *Eranos-Jahrbuch* 31 (1962): 117–69.

A discussion of the function of vision in Christian theology.

9   Boas, George. *Essays on Primitivism and Related Ideas in the Middle Ages.* Baltimore: Johns Hopkins University Press, 1948, pp. 154–74.

Study of "primitivism" which examines the idea of the earthly paradise using several examples, in particular the *Vision of Tundale, St. Patrick's Purgatory,* and *St. Brendan's Voyage.*

10   Boswell, C.S. *An Irish Precursor of Dante: A Study of the Vision of Heaven and Hell Ascribed to the Eighth Century Irish Saint Adamnán.* Grimm Library, 18. London: D. Nutt, 1908; rpt. New York, 1972.

See **23, 51**, and **210**. This book centers around the *Fis Adamnán* and provides an English translation. However, the major part of the book discusses in depth the classical, oriental, and ecclesiastical traditions of the otherworld visions; the *imrama* and *fis* in Irish literature and their development into later visions. The possibility of direct influence is unfounded, but Boswell claims that it is not unlikely that he was acquainted with several later works like the *Vision of Tundale*. Briefly includes *St. Patrick's Purgatory, Tundale* and *Brendan* in his discussion.

11   Carozzi, Claude. "La géographie de l'au-delà et sa signification pendant le haut Moyen-Age." *Popoli e paesi nella cultura altomedievale* (Settimana del Centro Italiano di Studi sull'Alto Medioevo) 29, 2 (1983): 423–81.

A study of visions of the otherworld between the sixth and early thirteenth century to determine the nature of geographical space and its relationship to the current symbolism of the otherworld and the idea of purgation and salvation.

12   Chiffoleau, Jacques. *La compatabilité de l'au delà: Les hommes, la morte et la religion dans la région de Avignon (1320–1480)*. Rome: École Française de Rome, 1980.

A fascinating study from the documentary evidence of the changing attitudes toward death and the afterlife during this period. Studies "the role of demographics and economics in the change of the imagery of 'passage' in the afterlife, the capacity of the church to control this radical change in the popular mentality, and the resulting transformation of the field of religion."

13   Ciccarese, Maria Pia. *Visioni dell'Aldilà in Occidente*. Florence: Nardini Editore, 1987.

Includes texts of important sources of otherworld vision literature, including, the *Apocalypse, Enoch, Visio Pauli,* the heavenly poetry of Prudentius, visions of the martyrs Perpetua and Saturo, the dream of Jerome, the

miracle of St. Martin, and the work of Augustine.
Includes the texts of Gregory the Great, Gregory of
Tours, the *Vision of Furseus,* the *Vision of Barontus,* the
Vision of Bonellus, Vision of Drythelm, selected letters of
Boniface, the *Life of St. Guthlac, Vision of a Poor
Woman,* and *Vision of Wetti,* all in Latin with facing
Italian translation. Includes several indexes, notes, and a
brief bibliography.

14   Dana, H. W. L. "Medieval Visions of the Other World."
        Cambridge, Ma.: Harvard University Dissertation,
        1910.

        Not seen.

15   Delepierre, Joseph Oct. *Livre des Visions.* London: p.
        unk., n.d.

        Not seen.

16   Dinzelbacher, Peter. *Vision und Visionsliteratur im
        Mittelalters.* Monagraphien zur Geschichte des
        Mittelalters 23. Stuttgart: Hiersemann, 1981.

        An exhaustive study on vision literature in the Middle
        Ages. Discusses previous research on and definitions of
        vision literature, and then examines the nature of visions;
        the space of the visions; the role of the visionary in
        relationship to space, motion, emotion, and time, and in
        relation to those met in the otherworld. Examines the
        relationship of allegory to vision literature. Concludes
        with a discussion of the function of the vision, its place in
        the life of the visionary, and the sociology of the
        visionary. Includes tables of visions pp. 13–23, 25–29.

17   ————. "Die Jenseitsbrücke im Mittelalter." Diss.:
          University of Vienna (104), 1973.

          A study of the motif of the bridge in literature of the
          otherworld. Includes, among others, Gregory the Great,
          *Adamnán, Esdrae, Alberic, Tundale, St. Patrick's
          Purgatory, Thurkill, St. Paul, William Staunton,* and
          Godeschalk.

18   ————. "Die Visionen des Mittelalters: Ein
          geschichtlicher Umriß." *Zeitschrift für Religions- und
          Geistesgeschichte* 30 (1978): S. 116–28.

          Examines the form, function, source, and spread,
          both in time and space, of vision literature, concluding
          that this type of literature is a special medieval form that
          could be more fruitfully examined as literary and religious
          history.

19   ————. "Klassen und Hierarchien im Jenseits."
          Miscellanea Mediaevalia 12 (1979): 20–40.

          Not seen.

20   ————. "Reflexionen irdischer Sozialstrukturen im
          mitteralterlishen Jenseits schilderungen." *Archiv fur
          Kulturgeschichte* 61 (1979): 16–34.

          Looks at heaven and hell in relation to Irish social
          structures.

21   ————. "La littérature des révélations au moyen âge: un
          document historique. *Revue Historique* 275 (1986):
          289–305.

          Not seen.

22 ——. "The Way to the Other World in Medieval Literature and Art." *Folklore* 97 (1986): 70–87.

A study of pictorial and allegorical interpretations of the soul's journey to the otherworld.

23 ——. *Mitteralterliche Visionsliteratur: Eine Anthologie.* Darmstadt: P. unk., 1989.

Not seen.

24 ——, and Harald Kleinschmidt. "Seelenbrücke und Brückenbau im mittelalterlichen England." *Numen* 31 (1984): 242–87.

An analysis of the relationship of the journey of the soul and the image of the bridge as it developed in vision literature in England in the Middle Ages.

25 Dod, Marcus. *Forerunners of Dante: An Account of Some of the More Important Visions of the Unseen World, from the Earliest Times.* Edinburgh: Clark, 1903.

Not seen.

26 Dünninger, Eberhard. "Politische und geschichtliche Elemente in mittelalterlichen Jenseitsvisionen bis zum Ende des 13. Jahrhunderts." Diss: Wurzburg, 1962.

Discusses the place of vision literature within the political context of the church, including both the bishops and the monastic orders. Includes bibliography.

27   Ebel, U. *Die Literarischen Formen der Jenseits- und Endzeitvisionen.* In *Grundriß der Romanischen Literatur des Mittlealters.* Edited by Hans Robert Jauss. vol. 6. Heidelberg: P. unk., 1968, 181–215.

        Not seen.

28   Erickson, Carolly. *The Medieval Vision. Essays in History and Perception.* New York: Oxford University Press, 1976.

        A study of the visionary world view in medieval life, describing how this view informed the sense of the universe. Erickson says that this is a view that we must understand and appreciate in order to recapture medieval perceptions of ideas and events.

29   Foster, Frances A. "Legends of the After-Life." In *A Manual of the Writings in Middle English: 1050–1500.* Ed. by J. Burke Severs and Albert E. Hartung. Hamden, CT: Connecticut Academy of Arts and Sciences, 1967–, 2: 452–57, 645–49.

        Description and bibliography on the Middle English *Vision of St. Paul, St. Patrick's Purgatory, Vision of Tundale, Vision of Fursey (Furseus), Vision of Leofric, Revelation of Purgatory by an Unknown Woman, Vision of the Monk of Eynsham.*

30   Fritzsche, C. "Die lateinischen Visionen des Mittelalters bis zur Mitte des 12. Jahrhunderts." *Romanische Forschungen* 2 (1886): 247–79; 3 (1887): 337–69.

        Presents a chronological discussion of the particular elements of specific visions from the sixth to the thirteenth century with focus on the cultural significance of these visions and on the particular elements. Chart (2:247–49) lists the visions discussed.

31   Fros, H. "Visionum medii aevi Latina repertorium." *The Use and Abuse of Eschatology in the Middle Ages.* Ed. by W. Verbeke, D. Verhelst and A. Wekenhysen. Louvain: Louvain University Press, 1988, 481–98.

        List with bibliographic citations.

32   Gardiner, Eileen. *Visions of Heaven and Hell before Dante.* New York: Italica Press, 1989.

        A collection of medieval visions of heaven and hell in English translation, including the visions of Charles the Fat, Drythelm, Furseus, the Monk of Eynsham, Paul, Tundale, and Thurkill; and *St. Brendan's Voyage* and *St. Patrick's Purgatory.* Includes a general introduction, notes, and bibliography.

33   Gardner, Tom C. "The Theater of Hell. A Critical Study of Some Twelfth-Century Latin Eschatological Visions." Ph.D. Diss.: University of California, Berkeley, 1976.

        Not seen.

34   Gatto, G. "Le Voyage au paradis: la christianisation des traditions folkloriques au Moyen Age." *Annales Economies, sociétés, civilizations* 34 (1979): 929–42.

        Using some examples, notably the *Lai of Guingamor,* discusses the elevation of oral tradition to the dignity of written culture: the passing of material from the lay vulgar language to Latin clerical literary productions.

35   Gurevich, A. J. "Popular and Scholarly Medieval
      Cultureal Tradition: Notes in the Margin of Jacques
      Le Goff's Book." *Journal of Medieval History* 9
      (1983): 71–90.

      Not seen.

36   ———. "The Divine Comedy before Dante." In *Medieval
      Popular Culture: Problems of Belief and Perception.*
      Trans. by János M. Bak and Paula A. Hollingsworth.
      Cambridge Studies in Oral and Literate Culture 14.
      Cambridge: Cambridge University Press, 1988. 104–
      52.

      Not seen.

37   Hellholm, D. *Das visionenbuch des Herman als
      Apocalypse. Formgeschichte und texttheoretische
      Studien zu einer literarischen Gattung.* Lund:
      Gleerup, 1980.

      Not seen.

38   Himmelfarb, Martha. *Tours of Hell: An Apocalyptic
      Form in Jewish and Christian Literature.*
      Philadelphia: University of Pennsylvania Press, 1983.

      Covers tours of hell from late antiquity to the fifth
      century, their background, and the traditions to which they
      gave rise. Uses parallels of sin/punishment pairs as
      crucial identifiers for clarifying the nature of the
      relationships among various texts. Covers, in addition to
      the Jewish texts, the following works, which are of
      interest in the context of the present volume: *Apocalypse
      of Peter, Apocalypse of Paul, Apocalypse of Mary,* and
      Vision of Ezra. Contains bibliography of editions and

translations of texts, bibliographies, and significant secondary literature.

39 Holdsworth, C. J. "Eleven Visions Connected with the Cistercian Monastery of Stratford Langthorne." *Cîteaux: Commentarii Cistercienses* 13 (1962): 185–208.

Presents Latin texts with brief introduction to Lambeth Palace 51, Peter of Cornwall's *Liber revelationum.*

40 ———. "Visions and Visionaries in the Middle Ages." *History* 48 (1963): 141–53.

In a rational approach, not limiting himself to visions of heaven and hell, Holdsworth discusses visions, which he attributes to a "medieval" frame of mind especially if suffering physical exhaustion (often through illness or fasting) and to the nature of the typical visionary and the vision recorder (amanuensis). Sees visions as providing insight into the political, social, and religious controversies of the period.

41 Hughes, Jonathan. *Pastors and Visionaries: Religion and Secular Life in Late Medieval Yorkshire.* Woodbridge: P. unk., 1988.

Not seen.

42 James, M. R. "Irish Apocrypha." *Journal of Theological Studies* 20 (1918): 9–16.

Discusses two Irish texts, *Evernew Tongue* and the *Vision of Adamnán,* pointing out similarities in their descriptions of the otherworld to apocalyptic literature, indicating some unknown work(s) of this genre as source for these Irish descriptions of otherworld.

43   Jodogne, Omer. "L'aurte monde celtique dans la littérature francaise du xiie siècle." *Bulletin de la classe des Lettres et des Sciences morales et politiques* of the Royal Academy of Brussels, ser. 5, 46 (1960): 584–97.

Analyzes the influence of Celtic concepts of the otherworld on French literature in an atmosphere receptive to ancient, Byzantine, Germanic, and Celtic concepts of the otherworld.

44   Kamphausen, Hans Joachim. *Traum und Vision in der Lateinischen Poesie der Karolingerzeit.* Bern and Frankfurt/M: Herbert Lang and Peter Lang, 1975.

Discusses the difference between dreams and visions in medieval literature and particularly Carolingian poetry with an emphasis on the development of the eschatological ideas of heaven, hell, and purgatory from the ancient to the Carolingian period. Shoaf describes this book as "a recent summary on the theological significance of this genre for communities which used and enjoyed it." Includes bibliography.

45   Kroll, J. *Gott und Höll: Der Mythos vom Descensus Kampke.* Kulturwissenschaftliche Bibliothek Warbur, Hamburg. Studien 20. Leipzig and Berlin: Tuebner, 1932.

A comparative study on descent into hell literature in the European Middle Ages (126–82) and in, among others, Egyptian, Babylonian Iranian, Indian, and Jewish cultures.

46   Le Goff, Jacques. "The Learned and Popular Dimensions
        of Journeys of the Otherworld in the Middle Ages."
        Translated by Victor Aboulaffia. In *Understanding
        Popular Cutlture*. Ed. by Steven L. Kaplan. New
        York: Mouton, 1984. Originally published in Le
        Goff's *L'imaginaire medievale*. Paris: Gallimard,
        1985.

        A discussion of the simultaneous influence of
        "popular" culture with its tendency "to spatialize spiritual
        life and to localize beliefs" and learned culture with its
        tendency to rationalize the beyond and domesticate
        narrative ramblings, in shaping the otherworld visions of
        the Middle Ages. Hypothesizes a four-part division:
        "before the seventh century, the Church's determination
        to destroy or occlude folkloric culture...."; "the seventh to
        the tenth centuries are the great era of visions of the
        beyond"...linked to growth of monasticism; "during the
        eleventh and twelfth centuries...folklore spreads the
        wisions widely"...linked to improved status of laity;
        "after twelfth century – learned culture's counter-
        attack...rationalizes the beyond and infernalizes the
        subterranean underworld."

47   Levison, Wilhelm. "Die Politik in Jenseitsvisionen des
        frühen Mittelalters." *Aus Rheinischer und frankischer
        Frühzeit*. Dusseldorf: L. Schwann, 1948, 229–46.

        Study of political aspects of early medieval vision
        literature with particular attention to the visions of Charles
        the Fat and Bernoldus.

48   Lieb, Michael. *The Visionary Mode*. Ithaca, N.Y.: Cornell
        University Press, 1991.

Explores the progressive acculturation of the visionary mode, tracing transfomations from its biblical origins through Judeo-Christian thought into the Middle Ages.

49   McCullough, J.A. *Early Christian Visions of the Other World.* Edinburgh: P. unk., 1912.

Not seen.

50   Monnier, J. *Le Descente aux Enfers. Etude de pensé religieuse d'art et de litterature.* Paris: Fischbacher, 1905.

Not seen.

51   Morgan, Alison. *Dante and the Medieval Otherworld.* Cambridge Studies in Medieval Literature 8. Cambridge: Cambridge University Press, 1990.

An excellent study of the relationship between the *Divine Comedy* and popular Christian belief regarding the otherworld based on the study of other visions of heaven and hell. Provides an appendix (pp. 211–33) listing medieval otherworld visions with background and bibliographic information.

52   Nutt, Alfred. "The Irish Vision of the Happy Otherworld and the Celtic Doctrine of Rebirth." In *The Voyage of Bran Son of Febal to the Land of the Living.* Ed and trans. by Meyer, Kuno. 2 vols. Grimm Library 4. London: D. Nutt, 1895, 1897, 1:101–331.

A comparative study of the otherworld in Celtic legend,with particular attention to the *imrama* (particularly the *Voyage of Bran*), the *Fis Adamnán,* and the *Vision of Paul,* with reference to biblical, Jewish, ancient, Scandinavian, Iranian, and Indian otherworlds.

53   Os, Arnold Barel van. *Religious Visions and the Development of Eschatological Elements in Medieval English Religious Literature.* Amsterdam: H. J. Paris, 1932.

Study of the sources for English vision literature, which lie in the universal fund of eschatological elements and probably reached England through the *Book of Enoch,* the *Apocalypse of Enoch,* the *Apocalypse of Peter,* and the *Vision of Paul.* Examines the influence of Islamic literature on later visions. Also studies the influence of English homilies, works of religious instruction and exempla. Includes reprints of the *Apocalypse of Peter* (262–64), *Vision of Paul* (264–66), and the *Vision of Adamnán* (266–74). Includes bibliography.

54   Owen, Douglas R. R. *The Vision of Hell: Infernal Journeys in Medieval French Literature.* New York: Barnes & Noble, 1971.

Discussion of French medieval accounts of hell and how in their treatments the authors disclose the general medieval idea of the Christian otherworld. Includes a diplomatic edition of the French text of the *Vision of Paul* from Dublin, Trinity College 951 Cl. I.5.19.

55   Ozanam, Antoine Frédéric. "Les Sources poétiques de la Divine Comédie." In *Les poètes franciscains en Italie au xiie siecle. Oeuvres complètes* 5. Paris: Lecoffre, 1872, 397–538.

Traces mostly ancient influence on Dante with some attention to medieval vision literature.

56   ———. *Dante e la philisophie catholique au XIII siecle.* Second ed. Paris: J. Lecoffre, 1845.

Discusses sources for the *D.C.*, concentrating on thirteenth-century poetry and ancient descents into hell-poetry. Includes a discussion on the originality of Dante.

57   Patch, Howard Rollin. "The Adaptation of Otherworld Motifs to Medieval Romance." *Philologica: The Malone Anniversary Studies.* Ed. by Thomas R. Kirby and Henry B. Woolf. Baltimore: Johns Hopkins University Press, 1949, 115–23.

Examines several romances to determine if and how otherworld motifs were introduced into them and what can, therefore, be inferred about the original plots of these romances.

58   ———. *The Other World According to Descriptions in Medieval Literature.* Cambridge, Ma.: Harvard University Press, 1950; reprint ed., New York: Octagon, 1970.

Discusses Oriental, Classical, Celtic, and Germanic prototypes for elements of the otherworld, especially paradise. Examines these elements in medieval vision literature, particularly the ascent, the river barrier or fiery river, the bridge, mountains as a barrier or general feature, the dark valley, and the wall as barrier. Also examines these motifs in medieval journey literature, allegories, and romances.

59   Peters, E. "Zur Geschichte der lateinischen Visionslegenden." *Romanische Forschungen* 8 (1896): 361–64.

Comments to supplement Fritzsche's article (000) on elements in various visions.

60   Petroff, Elizabeth Alvilda. *Medieval Women's Visionary Literature*. New York: Oxford University Press, 1986.

Introduction provides excellent study of the subject followed by selections of texts from twenty-eight women visionaries. Includes bibliography.

61   Piehler, Paul. *The Visionary Landscape: A Study in Medieval Allegory*. London: Arnold, 1971.

A very interesting work on a certain psychic experience with its literary result – allegory. Discusses the function of *loci* in allegory. Although not concerned specifically with otherworld visions, it provides important insights on visionary literature.

62   Rockelein, Hedwig. *Otloh, Gottschalk, Tnugdal: Individuelle und kollektive Visionsmuster des Hochmittelalters*. Europäische Hochschulschriften 3.319. Frankfurt/M and New York: Peter Lang, 1987.

Combines psychological and ethnological approach in a study of Otloh of Emmeran with particular reference to the "collective" visions of Gottschalk, Thurkill, Tundale, and Owein (*St. Patrick's Purgatory*).

63   ———, and Peter Dinzelbacher. "Verba hec tam mistica
          ex ore tam ydiote glebonis.: In *Volksreligion im
          hohen und späten Mittelalter.* Ed. By P. Dinzelbacher
          and D. Bauer. Paderborn: P. unk., 1989.

          Not seen.

64   Rüegg, August. *Die Jenseitsvorstellungen vor Dante und
          die übrigen literarischen Voraussetzungen der
          "Divine Commedia."* Ein quellenkritischer
          Kommentar. 2 vols. Einsiedeln/Cologne: Benziger,
          1945.

          A comparative study of visons of the otherworld
          including ancient and biblical, with medieval visions
          focusing in volume 1 on *Furseus* (pp. 292–95), *Laisren*
          (295–97,) *Drythelm* (297–308), *Barontus* (308–311),
          Wetti (311–13), the *imrama, Brendan* (327–31),
          Adamnán (332–51), *Tundale* (352–94), *St. Patrick's
          Purgatory* (Owein), (395–405), *Alberic* (406–34),
          Volume 2 concentrates on the influences of this literature
          on the *Divine Comedy.*

65   Seymour, St. John Drelincourt. "The Bringing Forth of
          the Soul in Irish Literature." *Journal of Theological
          Studies* 22 (1920): 16–20.

          Discusses a tradition in the literature of dying where
          the soul is unwilling or unable to leave the body through
          certain members (mouth, nose, etc.) either because they
          are sanctified (in the case of the righteous person) or are
          guarded by devils (in the case of sinners). Mentions two
          visions of the otherworld in this context, *Vision of St.
          Paul* and the *Vision of Ezra.*

66   ———. *Irish Visions of the Otherworld: A Contribution to the Study of Medieval Visions.* New York: Macmillan, 1930.

A study of the visions found in Irish ecclesiastical literature, the most striking feature of them being the change in their eschatology, which took place about the tenth century, which divides them into two classes. Discusses the visions of *Furseus, Laisrén, Adamnán, Drythelm, the Monk of Wenlock,* and *Tundale,* and the *Voyage of Brendan,* the vision of hell in the *Liber Flavus Fergusiorum* and the vision of heaven and hell in the *Voyage of the Húi Corra,* among others. Concludes that "in the earlier period the Celtic church in Ireland drew no distinction between hell and purgatory" until as a result of new ideas which culminated in the twelfth century Reformation, the doctrine of a purgatorial state distinct from hell emerged. Stated in the *Vision of Adamnán,* elaborated in the *Vision of Tundale,* and perfected in the vision of Owein.

67   ———. "Notes on Apocrypha in Ireland." *Proceedings of the Royal Irish Academy* 37c (1926): 107–16.

Study of the knowledge of eastern and western apocrypha in Ireland and its influence on early Irish literature.

68   ———. "The Seven Heavens in Irish Literature." *Zeitschrift für celtische Philologie* 14 (1923): 18–30.

Examines the Irish tradition of the seven heavens as described in Irish literature, including the *Vision of Adamnán* and the *Vision of Tundale,* and briefly touches on some non-Irish visions.

69   ———. "The Eschatology of the Early Irish Church."
          Zeitschrift für celtische Philologie 14 (1923): 179–
          211.

          An account of the views held by the early Irish
          church on the otherworld and particularly on the
          development of the purgatorial doctrine. Discusses both
          imrama and visions (Furseus, Laisrén Adamnán, and
          Tundale; plus non-Irish Drythelm and the Monk of
          Wenlock). Covers heaven, hell, division of souls, fire of
          doom, and purgatory. He argues that before the ninth
          century the Irish church conceived of hell as a place from
          which souls could be released through the intervention of
          a saint or the pious deeds of the living. From the tenth
          century purgatory becomes separate from hell and the
          later Irish visions describe a separate purgatorial state –
          reflecting a view more in line with orthodoxy and
          probably related to the revolution in ecclesiastical matters
          taking place in Ireland before the close of the twelfth
          century.

70   Silverstein, Théodore. "Dante and the Legend of the
          Mi'raj: The Problem of Islamic Influence on the
          Christian Literature of the Otherworld." *Journal of
          Near Eastern Studies* 11 (1952): 89–110, 187–97.

          Calls for a reexamination of the influence of Islamic
          literature on Christian literature of the otherworld.

71   Thompson, Stith. "Otherworld Journeys." In *Motif-Index
          of Folk Literature*. Ed. by Stith Thompson. Rev. ed.
          Bloomington, Ind.: Indiana University Press, 1955–
          58, 3:7–37.

          Motif index.

72   Villari, Pasquale. *Antiche leggende e traduzione che
      illustrano la* Divina Commedia *precedute da alcune
      osservazioni.* Pisa: Nistri, 1865. Also in *Annali delle
      Università Toscane* 8 (1866): 1–162; rpt. 1979.

      Introduction on Dante and his predecessors. Presents
      editions of *Tundale* (Latin and Italian), *St. Patrick's
      Purgatory* (Italian), *St. Paul* (Italian), and *St. Brendan's
      Voyage* (Italian).

73   Willson, Elizabeth. "The Middle English Legends of
      Visits to the Other World and their Relation to the
      Metrical Romances." Ph.D. Diss.: University of
      Chicago, 1917.

      Study of the crossover between romance and legend
      in phraseology and meter. Primarily attempts to show that
      the material was common to both forms and only
      secondarily was there influence of romances on writers of
      legends. Traces early influences on visions. Discusses *St.
      Paul, Tundale, Monk of Eynsham, St. Patrick's
      Purgatory,* and the *Voyage of St. Brendan,* plus the
      "Falmouth Squire," and two other works.

74   Zaleski, Carol. *Otherworld Journeys: Accounts of Near-
      Death Experience in Medieval and Modern Times.*
      New York and Oxford: Oxford University Press,
      1987.

      An excellent book that examines the medieval visions
      of heaven and hell and links them to contemporary
      accounts of near-death experiences to provide an
      understanding of these visions as religious and
      imaginative experiences. Good bibliography.

THE VISION OF ADAMNÁN (FÍS ADAMNÁIN)

A vision of heaven and hell erroneously attributed to Adamnán (625?–704 CE), abbot of Hy and Iona, biographer of St. Columba. Middle Irish. Part One (sections 1–20) dates from the eleventh century; Part Two (sections 21–30) from early tenth. The work appears in two famous Irish manuscripts, both in the Royal Irish Academy, Dublin: *The Book of the Dun Cow* and The Speckled Book, and two other manuscripts. This work, which is approximately 500 words long, shows the influence of the *Seven Heavens Apocryphon,* the *Vision of Paul,* and the writings of Gregory the Great.

On the feast of John the Baptist, Adamnán is said to be conveyed to the otherworld, where his guardian angel leads him first on a tour of heaven, of the Land of the Saints and then on a tour of hell. There is a description of the Glorious One seated upon a throne and of the music and fragrance that envelopes this scene in the seven-walled heavenly city. There is also a city inhabited by those not yet ready for the heavenly city. This city has six doors where all are confronted on their way to heaven, and some are forced to remain for periods of time to be prepared for the heavenly city. This is obviously a prototype of Christian purgatory.

Finally, the unworthy souls are sent to hell into the hand of Lucifer. There are several different types of punishment, for a variety of sinners, including those who abused their religious office, but, in general, there is a wide array of sinners whose sins are not particularly described. There is a fiery wall beyond the land of torment, where only devils now dwell, but which will be open to all after the Day of Judgment. Adamnán is led back to heaven and is prepared to remain, but is sent back to earth to tell both laymen and religious what he has seen. The vision is told in the third person, and the character of Adamnán is seldom mentioned.

23

There is no interaction between the visionary and the other characters in this vision.

Sources[1]
75   *Leabhar Braec. The Speckled Book.* Dublin: Royal Irish
        Academy, 1876, 2:253–56.

        Facsimile of Leabhar Braec (The Speckled Book)
        manuscript, containing the Celtic text of the *Vision of
        Adamnán.*

76   *Leabhar na H-Uidhri. The Book of the Dun Cow.* Ed. by
        Moelmuiri Mac Ceileachair. Dublin: Royal Irish
        Academy, 1870, 27–31.

        Facsimile of Leabhar na H-Uidhri (The Book of the
        Dun Cow) manuscript. Introduction provides a
        description of the manuscript, containing the Celtic text of
        the *Vision of Adamnán.*

77   *Leabhar na H-Uidhri. The Book of the Dun Cow.* Ed. by
        Richard I. Best and Osborn Bergin. Dublin: Royal
        Irish Academy, 1929, 67–76.

        Facsimile of Leabhar na H-Uidhri (The Book of the
        Dun Cow) manuscript, containing the Celtic text of the
        Vision of Adamnán.

78   Boswell, see **10,** pp. 28–47.

        Introduction on the historical Adamnán and his
        relationship to this text. Discusses briefly the two

---

1. According to Dumville **(87),** p. 62, a new edition of this work was
being prepared by Professor. J. E. Caerwyn Williams, but I have not
been able to determine whether it has been published.

manuscripts. Provides an English translation of the Dun Cow text, Leabhar na H-Uidhri.

79   Colwell, James Joseph. "Fis Adamnán: A Comparative Study, with Introduction, Text, and Commentary based on the verision of the Lebor na Huidre." Ph.D. Diss.: University of Edinburgh, 1952.

    Not seen.

80   dá Cherda, Mac, see **83**.

81   Os, see **53**, pp. 266–74.

    Reprint of Boswell (see **10**) translation.

82   Stokes, Margaret, see **83**.

83   Stokes, Whitley. *Fis Adamnain.* Simla, 1870.

    Original not seen, but it includes an annotated transcription and translation from the Book of the Dun Cow. The annotated translation, in which "everything has been sacrificed to literalness," is reprinted, under name of Mac dá Cherda, in *Fraser's Magazine* 83, n.s. 3: (1871): 184–94, with a very brief introduction covering mss, language, and date, followed by the English translation (includes notes of a general literary kind); and reprinted from Fraser's, with a few corrections and additions, in Margaret Stokes, *Three Months in the Forests of France.* (London: G. Bell, 1895), 265–79.

84   ———. "Adamnan's Second Vision." *Revue celtique* 12 (1891): 420–43.

Taken from the lithographic facsimile of the Leabhar Braec (158b–159b), an edition of a second version of the *VA* in Irish, preceded by four Latin paragraphs, with facing English translation, notes and a brief glossary of unusual Irish words.

85   Vendryes, Joseph. "Aislingthi Adhamnáin d'après le texte du manuscrit de Paris." *Revue celtique* 30 (1909): 349–83.

Presents diplomatic edition of Irish text of the B. N. Paris MS. Fond celtique no. 1 (fifteenth century) with facing French translation. The text of this manuscript is more closely related to the Dun Cow text.

86   Windisch, Ernst, ed. "Fis Adamnáin; Die Vision des Adamnán." *Irische Texte* 1(1880): 165–96.

Brief introduction on manuscripts, language, and dating. Presents diplomatic editions of two of the three manuscripts: Leabhar na H-Uidhri (Book of the Dun Cow, c. 1100) and Leabhar Braec (The Speckled Book, late fourteenth century), both from the Royal Irish Academy, Dublin.

Studies
87   Dumville, D. N. "Towards an Interpretation of the *Fís Adamnán*." *Studia celtica* 12–13 (1977–78): 62–77.

Details editions, translations, and manuscripts, and then proceeds to examine earlier treatments of the text in terms of the eschatology evidenced in the work. Discusses the relationship between the *FA* and the *Visio Pauli*. Concludes that the author combined a number of sources with very different backgounds of eschatological thought, which he managed to reconcile into a coherent work.

88   James, M. R. "Syriac Apocrypha in Ireland." *Journal of Theological Studies* 11 (1910): 290–91.

Briefly discusses a link between the *VA* and the Syriac apocryphal work, *Obsequies of the Holy Virgin* — the clearest evidence James had yet "encountered of obligation on the part of an Irish writer to an oriental text.

89   ———. "Irish Apocrypha," see **42**.

Discusses two Irish texts, *Evernew Tongue* and the *Vision of Adamnán,* pointing out similarities in their descriptions of the otherworld to apocalyptic literature, indicating some unknown work(s) of this genre as source for these Irish descriptions of otherworld.

90   Kenney, James F. *The Sources for the Early History of Ireland: Ecclesiastical. An Introduction and Guide.* New York: Columbia University Press, 1929; rev. and rpt. New York: Octagon Books, 1966, 444–45.

Brief discussion of the text, list of mss, and a bibliography up to 1929.

91   Seymour, St. John Drelincourt. "The Vision of Admanan." *Proceedings of the Royal Irish Academy* 37c.15 (1927): 304–12.

Analysis of VA in its four surviving texts, as a composite work of two main divisions, as Boswell (**10**) charted them (sections 1–20, 31 and perhaps 32 to end; and 21–30). The first is based on a four-fold division of souls immediately after death with a description of the ascent of two classes through the seven heavens; the second is a supplement describing the unpleasant side of the otherworld, which Seymour sees as at odds with the rest of the work presenting unsolved problems.

THE VISION OF AILSI

This vision was recorded by Peter of Cornwall in his *Liber revelationum* (Bk. 1, ch. 6: 13–17). Ailsi is Peter's grandfather, who experienced a series of visions, culminating in a vision of the otherworld, which he experienced after the death of his son, Pagan.

Pagan leads his father through a nocturnal vision of the otherworld, teaching him about the otherworld and acting as his guide. This vision seems strongly influenced by the visions of Furseus, Drythelm, and Paul, as well as by *St. Patrick's Purgatory*. This influence may be the result of Peter's knowledge of these works rather than the description Peter received from his grandfather.

Ailsi is taken first through purgatory, and he descends into a dark valley, where he searches for a bridge to enable him to cross a river, however, not finding the bridge he is flown over on Pagan's back, crossing both a river of fire and ice. Souls are punished with gradual immersion as is found in other visions. There is also a house full of torments. Pagan and Aisli next visit the valley of hell where souls rise and fall in flames. Aisli also visits the earthly paradise, a broad field where souls patiently await entrance into heaven.

At the end of the vision Aisli asks to remain with Pagan, but is warned to return and the vision immediately fades.

Sources

92   Easting, Robert, and Richard Sharpe, ed. "Peter of Cornwall: 'The Visions of Ailsi and his Sons.'" *Mediaevistik* 1 (1988): 207– 63.

Study of Peter of Cornwall's treatment of the series of visions experienced by Ailsi, with information on

Peter, his life and writings, mss of his writings, his sources, and the Cornish background of his work. Presents Latin edition of the text from the Lambeth Palace Library 51.

93   Sharpe, Richard, and Peter Hull, ed. and trans. *Cornish Studies* 13 (1985).

Not seen. Edition and translation of text.

THE VISION OF ALBERIC

Alberic of Settefrati (b. c. 1100) was a monk of Monte Cassino under Gerard (1111–23). His vision, at the age of ten, was written down in 1121–23 by Guido, a priest of the Abbey of Monte Cassino; his work was corrected by Alberic, under Abbot Senioretto, with the help of Peter the Deacon in 1127–37. Primary focus of criticism has been on its relation to the Divine Comedy. The sole ms, of about 7000 words, is Monte Cassino 257, fol. 712–34. This work bears traces of the influence of the visions of Perpetua, Wetti, Furseus, and the *Voyage of Brendan*, texts which were present in the library.

There is a prologue to the vision explaining how Alberic was obliged to revise his account of the vision, because so much extraneous material had been added to it.

The vision begins with Alberic lying sick, as if dead, for nine days. Peter and two angels, Emmanuel and Hélos, act as his guides. Hell is visited first. It is a series of locations, each dedicated to a particular group of sinners. There is a river of purgatory. Alberic is eventually shown the seven heavens and a land beyond, of which he is not permitted to speak. He is shown the fifty-one provinces of earth before he is finally returned to his body when Peter tells him to remember to make an offering each year at his church.

Source

94   *Bibliotheca Casinensis* 5, 1 (1894): 191–206.

        Latin edition. Not seen.

95   de Vivo, Catello. *La Visione di Alberico ristampata, tradotta, e comparata con la Divina Commedia.* Ariano: Appula-Irpino, 1899.

Unannotated diplomatic edition of Latin text followed by Italian translation. Introduction in Italian focuses on similarities between the *VA* and the *Divine Comedy* with extensive quotes from the latter.

96   Inguanez, Mauro, ed. "La Visione di Alberico." Introduction by Antonio Mirra. *Miscellanea Casinense* 11 (1931–32): 33–103.

Contains an edition of this vision (pp. 83–103). Not seen.

97   Marchand, Jean. *L'autre monde au Moyen Age.* Poèmes et récits de la vielle France 17. Paris: Boccard, 1940, 117–83.

Includes brief historical introduction plus a bibliography of editions and selected studies, a brief description of the manuscript at Monte Cassino, and a French translation of text. Also includes the *Voyage of St. Brendan* and *St. Patrick's Purgatory.*

98   Saint-Victor, P. "La vision du frere Alberic." *Correspondant* 8 (1844): 214–37.

Brief introduction followed by a complete French translation of Latin text with notes making comparisons to the *Divine Comedy*, focusing on Dante's possible knowledge of Alberic's vision.

Studies
99   Ancona, Alessandro D', see **3**, pp. 3–66.

Treats the antecedents of Dante in general and gives some particular attention to the Paul, Brendan Tundale, Patrick and Alberic visions. He does not make firm connections between these and the *Divine Comedy,* but indicates a general millieu of vision literature, which does not detract from Dante's originality.

100   Dinzelbacher, Peter. "Die 'Vision Alberichs' und die 'Esdras-Apokryphe.'" *Studien und Mitteilungen zur Geschichte des Benediktiner-ordens und seine Zweige* 87 (1976): 435–42.

Discusses the VA in the context of apocryphal literature and especially the *Visio Ezra,* with a brief textual comparison.

101   Guerico, Luigi. *Di alcuni rapporti tra le visioni medievali e la Divina Commedia.* Rome: P. unk., 1909.

Not seen.

102   Lauri, Achille. "Dei due Alberici da Settefrati, Monaci di Montecassino." *Rivista storica benedettina* 6 (1911): 208–20.

Distinguishes the monk Alberic of Settefrati (b. 1101) from the cardinal Alberic of Settefrati (b. 1008). Also discusses the influence of this vision on the *Divine Comedy.*

103   Ovidio, Francisco d'. *Nuovi studi danteschi. Il Purgatorio.* Milan: Hoepli, 1906, 433–69.

In the context of Dante's "Purgatorio" Ovidio discusses the non-eternal nature of punishment in the VA; also discusses the *Vision of Tundale* in this context.

104   Rasetti, Gerardo. "Die Vision Alberichs in einem Frasko des 13 Jahrhunderts." *L'illustrazione Vaticana* 4(2)/Jg. 1933, 103ss.

Not seen.

105   Torraca, F. *Opere minori di Dante Alighieri.* Florence: Sansoni, 1906, 311–40.

Not seen.

THE VISION OF ANSELLUS SCHOLASTICUS or VISION OF A CERTAIN MONK IN THE MONASTERY OF ST. REMIGIO (VISIO CUJUSDAM MONACHI IN MONASTERIO S. REMIGII, DESCRIPTA AB ANSELLO, DISCIPULO S. ABBONIS, ABBATIS FLORIACENSIS, JUSSU ODDONIS ABBATIS)

Written by a monk of Auxerre, Ansellus of Rheims, *scholasticus,* of Fleury, in Latin verse by order of Odon, abbot of Saint-Germain d'Auxerre. Older prose version dates from between 1032 and 1052; version in octosyllabic couplets is of a later but uncertain date. It is suggested that the vision was experienced by Odon himself. (Length: approximately 2000 words.)

This vision begins with the story of Clovis and St. Remigius before going on to tell of the monk who, after traveling to Rheims at the Kalends of October, the feast of St. Remigio, dreams that he is preaching in the church at Easter and then is taken with Christ on the harrowing of hell. When sent back to earth through hell, since he was not yet to be taken into heaven, he is guided by a devil who protects him from the demons threatening him. This devil follows him all the way back to earth and climbs into bed with him to hold a series of discussions relating to the harrowing of hell. The vision ends with a humorous exchange about the monastic custom, which the devil finds offensive, of rising early for morning office.

This vision is unusual in its focus on the specific incident of the harrowing which is also related in the *Gospel of Nicodemus,* a possible influence in this vision, and in the devil playing the role of guide.

Sources

106   Du Méril, Edelestand, ed. *Poésies populaires latines antérieures au douzième siècle.* Paris: Brockhaus et Avenarius, 1843, 200–17.

Edition of Latin text with notes.

107   Leclerq, Jean. "Une rédaction en prose de la 'Visio Anselli Scholastici' dans un manuscrit de Subiaco." *Benedictina* 16 (1969): 188–95.

Edition of Latin text with introduction that briefly describes the vision, compares the prose and verse versions, and confirms Wilmart's thesis (see **113**) regarding the dedicatee of the vision .

108   PL 151:643–52.

Reprint of Du Méril (see **106**).

Studies

109   Ermini, Filippo. "La 'Visio Anselli' e l'imitazione nella 'Divina Commedia.'" *Medioevo Latini: Studi e ricerche.* Ed. Filippo Ermini. Modena: P.Unk., 1938, 311–15.

Not seen

110   Shoaf, Richard A. "Raoul Glaber et la 'Visio Anselli Scholastici.'" *Cahiers de Civilization Médiévale* 23 (1980): 215–19.

Discusses the relationship of the two versions of the *VAS* with the vision of the Harrowing of Hell in Book 5 (after 1044) of the *Historiarum libri cinque* of Raoul Glauber (monk of St. Germain d'Auxerre from 1035).

111   ———. "The *Visio Anselli Scholastici.* Exegesis and the
          Frustration of Aethiop." *Mittellateinisches Jahrbuch*
          17 (1982): 46–50.

          Discusses how the devil's frustrating role as the one
          who enlightens is treated with humor in the *VAS.*

112   Walther, Hans. *Initia carminum ac versum medii aevi
          posterioris latinorum.* Gottingen: Vandenhoeck &
          Ruprecht, 1959, p. 459, entry 9091.

          List of manuscripts and editions.

113   Wilmart, André. "La lettre-préface de la 'Visio Anselli
          Scholastici.'" *Analecta Reginensia.* Vatican City:
          Vatican Library, 1933, 283–85.

          Discusses the light that this letter from Ansellus to
          Odon, abbot of St. Germain sheds on our understanding
          of the writing of this vision. Presents a critical edition of
          the letter based on Vatican Reg. Lat. 73, fol. 56v and two
          additional mss.

THE VISION OF ST. ANSGAR

Late ninth century. This vision is part of the life of St. Ansgar, archbishop of Bremen and Hamburg (801–65), of which two versions, both in Latin, exist: one in prose by St. Rimbert (d. 888), Anskar's successor; and the other in verse by Gualdo (1065), Rimbert's successor. Rimbert's version of the vision appears in chapter 3 of his *Life of St. Ansgar*, of which there are many editions; a selection is included below.

The vision occurs on Pentecost when this holy young monk is visited by St. Peter and St. John the Baptist, both of whom he recognizes immediately. He is taken first to the fire of purgatory where, left alone, he suffers for three days. At one point, while undergoing this torment, he loses all memory. He is then rejoined by his guides and led to view from afar the land of the saints where The Lord appears in the east. Ansgar sees here the twenty-four elders. The description of heaven is mainly one of great brightness and singing and of the saints as sitting although incorporeal. The voice of God sends Ansgar back to life where he is supposed to be "crowned with martyrdom." He is led back by his guides as instantaneously as he was brought. His description, he says, is limited by the pen which "can in no way express all of which the mind is conscious."

Sources

114   AS 3(Feb. 1) : 409–500.

       Edition of Latin text.

115   MGH SRG 2: 690–92.

       Critical edition of Latin text by C. F. Dahlmann with brief introduction concerning mss and editions.

116   PL 18:962–64.

      Latin edition of St. Rimbert's *Vita Anskarii,* from Mabillion, *AB* 6.

117   Robinson, Charles H., ed. *Anskar, Apostle of the North 801–865.* London: Society for the Propagation of the Gospel, 1921, 30–34.

      English translation of the *Vita,* which contains the *Visio* in ch. 3. Includes a bibliography on the *Vita,* with information on mss on p. 21; bibliography on pp. 22–24.

118   Trillmich, W. "Vita Anskarii." In *Quellen des 9 and 11 Jahrhunderts zur Geschichte der Hamgburgischen Kirche and des Reiches.* Ed. by R. Buchner. Darmstadt: P. unk., 1961, 3–133.

      Not seen. Edition of text by Rimbert.

119   Waitz, G., ed. *Rimbert's Vita Anskarii.* Hannover: Scriptores rerum Germanicarum, 1884.

      Discusses the mss and early editions in preface. Presents annotated, critical edition of Rimbert's Latin text.

Studies

120   Haupt, Richard, see **123.**

121   Lammars, Walther. "Ansgar: Visionäre Erlebnisformen und Missionauftrag." *Speculum historiale.* (Festschrift for Johannes Spörl). Ed. by Clemens Bauer, et al. Freiburg: K. Alber, 1965, 541–58.

      Study of the relationship between Ansgar as visionary and as missionary.

122 Levison, Wilhelm, see **123**.

123 Mehnert, G. "Ansgar als Visionär, Ein Beitrag zur Geschichte des christlichen Vision des Frühmittelalters." *Schriften des Vereins für Schleswig-Holsteinische Kirchengeschichte,* 2 (Beiträge und Mitteilungen) 21 (1965): 44–67.

Examines the wider meaning of Ansgar as visionary, discussing twelve different visions occurring in the *Vita Anskarii* (in chs. 2–5, 9, 25, 27, 29, 35, 36, 38 and 40), with a recapitulation of previous scholarship, especially discussing related articles by Richard Haupt (*Schriften des Vereins für Schleswig-Holsteinische Kirchengeschichte* 2 (1926): 236–58) and Wilhelm Levison (*Schriften des Vereins für Schleswig-Holsteinische Kirchengeschichte,* 2 (1926): 163–65) on the *Vita* and the place of visions in this historical document.

THE VISION OF BALDARIUS (DE COELESTI REVELATIONE FACTA BALDARIO)

A brief Latin vision of heaven in about 50 words written by Saint Valerius del Bierzo, Benedictine abbot of St. Pedro de Montes (Léon, Spain, fl. 675–95). Valerius is also the author of the *Vision of Bonellus* and the *Vision of Maximus*. The *VB* is included in books 23–24 (656 CE)of his *Opere*.

At the time of St. Fructuosus of Braga (d. 665), a young slave who was a stone mason was taken sick and during his illness he was brought to heaven by three doves, who brought him into an enormous gathering of people in white, in front of which sat Christ enthroned, whom Baldarius does not immediately recognize. Christ tells Baldarius's guides to return him to earth since his time is not yet come, but he delays them because he is afraid Baldarius will be burned by the rising sun, which is poetically described, down to the enormous red bird whose flapping wings cool the intense heat. Baldarius is finally returned to earth, describing his reentry as if he were landing in a spaceship.

Sources
124   Ciccarese, see **13**, pp. 292–97.

Latin text based on Pousa (**126**) with facing Italian translation. Includes brief introduction (276–79) on the nature of this work with regard to the others in the collection. Provides some notes (298–301) to the text.

125   PL 87, 435–36.

Reprint of the diplomatic edition of the Latin text edited by Henrique Flórez et al., in *Espana sagrada*, 51 vols. (Madrid: Gabriel Ramirez, 1762) 16:385–87.

126   Pousa, Ramon Fernández, ed. *San Valerio: Edicion critica con XIII facsimiles.* Madrid: Instituto Antonio de Nebrija, 1942, 119–21.

Critical edition. Not seen.

Studies
127   Aherne, Consuelo Maria, ed. *Valerio of Bierzo: An Ascetic of the Late Visigothic Period.* Washington, D.C.: Catholic University Press, 1949, 57–61.

Includes a brief discussion of the three visions (Baldarius, Bonellus, and Maximus) with comparison to Valerio's autobiographical writings and to each other. Each of the visions is apparently related to Valerio by the visionary himself. Claims that "the accounts of the three visions are among the most interesting of Valerio's writings." Includes a general, select bibliography on Valerio.

THE VISION OF BARONTUS (VISIO BARONTI MONACHI LONGORETENSIS)

The *Vision of Barontus* is an eighth-century Latin prose vision of heaven and hell approximately 4700 words long. Vision itself dated 25 March 678 or 679, and the author claims to be the visionary in what is one of the more fascinating and dramatic visions of the otherworld.

Barontus, a monk in the monastery of St. Peter at Longoreto (Saint-Cyran near Bourges), who has repented of his past life and joined a monastery, falls ill. His fellow monks keep watch over him while his soul has left his body. When he finally recovers, he is asked to tell of his vision, which he then proceeds to do, explaining how he was immediately beset by devils who wanted to take him to hell, but he was protected by the angel Raphael who brought him on a journey through heaven where he might be judged before the devils made off with him.

Barontus and Raphael visit four levels of heaven, and Barontus repeatedly meets there people he has known, especially monks from his monastery, while the devils keep up a constant tug-of-war for Barontus. Finally Raphael sends another angel to bring St. Peter to them. Peter arrives and asks the devils what charges they have against this soul, and they charge Barontus with having three wives. Barontus admits to the charge, but the devils had by now become so annoying to everyone that Peter whacks them with his keys and sends them scurrying. He then decides to send Barontus back to earth via hell, so that Barontus can consider reforming his life.

Needing a guide, Frannoaldo is chosen on the condition that Barontus take particular care of this soul's tomb near the door of their church. They leave heaven with Barontus warned to give a certain sum to the poor and to protect himself with the phrase "Gloria a te, O Dio." In hell he sees sinners of every kind, all joined together suffering. Although the terrain of hell is not carefully described, the souls that Barontus meets who are suffering in hell are mentioned. Finally Barontus returns to his cell where he speaks with his fellow monks.

The vision closes with a statement by the author, allegedly Barontus, attesting to the veracity of this vision.

Sources
128   AS 3 March 25, 570–74.

         Edition of Latin vision preceded by commentary (567–69).

129   Ciccarese, see **13**, pp. 236–75

         Latin text based on MGH (**130**) with facing Italian translation. Includes brief introduction on the nature of this work with regard to the others in the collection. Provides some notes to the text.

130   MGH, Scriptores Merovingian 5: 368–94.

         Annotated critical edition of Latin text. Introduction by W. Levison includes discussion of mss, brief description of vision, comparison to other visions.

Studies
131   Ciccarese, Maria Pia. "La 'Visio Baronti' nella tradizione letteraria delle visiones dell'aldilá." *Romano Barbarica* 6. Rome: Herder, 1981–82, 25–52.

         Discusses the vision genre as related to the visions in the *Dialogues* of Gregory the Great and beginning in the seventh century. Describes the *VB* as a more original vision displaying imagination and narrative talent, while preserving the traditional style and themes of this genre.

THE VISION OF BERNOLDUS (DE VISIONE BERNOLDI PRESBYTERI)

This late ninth-century Latin vision of hell (in about 1600 words) is attributed to Hincmar (806–82), archbishop of Rheims.

After four days lying sick, Bernoldus lay as if dead, but he revived in the middle of the night to tell his vision to a priest. He described how he was led from this world to another where he met several people who were known to him. Each of these individuals or groups asked Bernoldus to help them in their suffering by appealing to their followers to pray and perform charitable works in their names. Among those he meets are forty-one archbishops; and the bishops Ebo, archbishop of Rheims, Leopardus, and Aeneus. He later meets King Charles the Bald, a man named Jesse, and a Count Otharius, who tried to hide from Bernoldus. He helps to ease the pain of each and propel them on to paradise. One of the most interesting features of this vision is the mention of several other visions as precedents for the veracity of this type of story. Mentioned specifically are the *Dialogues* of Gregory; Bede's *Historia,* which includes the visions of Furseus and Drythelm; the letters of Boniface, which includes the *Vision of the Monk of Wenlock*; and the *Vision of Wetti.* Bernoldus has an unnamed guide for a brief period. The otherworld landscape is undistinguished, although mixed between places of great beauty and places of putridness. The importance of aiding the dead through alms, prayers and Masses is a primary theme of this vision.

Sources
132   PL 125:1115–19.

   Edited from a codex of the monastery of Herivallensis.

Studies

133   Levison, Wilhelm, see **437**.

Study of political aspects of early medieval vision literature with particular attention to the visions of Charles the Fat and Bernoldus.

THE VISION OF BONELLUS (DE BONELLO MONACHO CUI REVELATIO INFERNI FACTA EST)

A brief Latin vision, of about 700 words, written by Saint Valerius del Bierzo (see *Vision of Baldarius*) in books 20–22 of his *Opere*.

Bonellus, a Spanish monk of the eleventh century, tells Valerio directly how an angel brought him up to heaven and showed him a dwelling richly built with gems and pearls. He is promised a place here after he dies, but in the meantime he is brought to hell where devils lead him from precipice to precipice. Here he meets a young boy whom he had known, who intercedes with the devils for Bonellus. He is shown the devil, the pit of hell, and three giants, called bad angels. At a lake of fire, archers shoot arrows at him until he makes the sign of the cross and is rescued from hell, and returned to this world, where he undertakes to lead an exemplary life.

Sources
134   Ciccarese, see **13**, pp. 286–92.

       Latin text based on Pousa (**136**) with facing Italian translation. Includes brief introduction (276–79) on the nature of this work with regard to the others in the collection. Provides some notes (298–301) to the text.

135   PL 87: 433–35.

       Reprint of the diplomatic edition of the Latin text edited by Henrique Flórez et al., in *Espana sagrada*, 51 vols. (Madrid: Gabriel Ramirez, 1762), 16:382–85.

136   Pousa, see **126**, pp. 115–18.

Critical edition. Not seen.

Studies
137   Aherne, see **127**.

Brief discussion of the three visions (Baldarius, Bonellus, and Maximus) with comparison to Valerio's autobiographical writings and to each other. Each of the visions is apparently related to Valerio by the visionary himself. Claims that "the accounts of the three visions are among the most interesting of Valerio's writings." Includes a general, select bibliography on Valerio.

THE VISION OF BOSO OF DURHAM (QUALIA BOSO MILES DE CENOBITIS DUNELMENSIBUS VIDERIT...)

This brief Latin vision is included in *The History of the Church of Durham* (Bk. 4, ch. 9) of Simeon of Durham for 1095. Boso, a knight of the bishop falls ill and for three days lies as if dead. During his vision, he is warned to first confess and undertake repentance and then to reveal what he has seen to his prior. He witnesses a procession of monks, proceeding toward a high wall without gate. Unlike other visionaries who are transported over the wall, he finds a little window and within sees a wide field of flowers where he recognizes many monks from Durham.

Among the monks previously seen were two headed in the wrong direction, and Boso is told to tell the prior of his monastery about them, and warn him to be sure that the monks are all confessed and following the right path.

Next he sees English soldiers, all of whom are condemned to hell and vanish like a puff of smoke and Norman knights who vanish into a hole in the earth, indicating that to this author warriors are category of sinners and not an unfortunate necessity. There is a condemnation of married priests and finally a warning to bishop William, predicting his and his successor's early deaths, and warning all to diligently repent.

The author concludes with a testimony to the truth of this vision, stating that all that Boso predicted was fulfilled.

Sources
138   Simeon of Durham. *Historia Dunelmensis Ecclesiae*. Ed.
       by Thomas Arnold, ed. Rolls Series 75/1: 130–32.
       London: Public Record Office: 1882–85.

       Diplomatic edition of Latin text.

THE VISION OF THE BOY WILLIAM

A brief vision of hell and heaven (dated 1146, in approximately 600 words) by a fifteen-year old boy named William. The vision lasts five days; on the third day he is seen to make the sign of the cross, which he does before leaving hell; and on the fifth day he revives after seeing heaven.

He has a guide through the otherworld, where he sees both fire and ice used in the punishments of hell. Tortures include rivers of ice cold water, fires, a flaming wheel, and a field where sinners are suspended above temptations that they cannot reach. He sees the mouth of hell and receives a strong warning before being abandoned temporarily by his guide who soon returns to take him through the apparently impenetrable wall of paradise. They enter a twelve-gated, round building where he moves among the blessed and is promised a place should he manage to live a good life. He also is shown another William, a boy who was crucified by the Jews and so enjoys great honor as a martyr in heaven.

This vision is found in the *Speculum Historiale* of Vincent of Beauvais (d. 1264). It may have been influenced by the visions of Paul and Drythelm and makes specific reference to the *Apocalypse.*

Sources
139   Vincent of Beauvais. *Bibliotheca mundi seu Speculi maioris.* Vol. 4, *Speculum historiale.* Douay: B. Belleri, 1624; rpt. ed. Graz: Akademische Druck-u. Verlagsanstalt, 1965, 1125–26.

Book 27, ch. 84–85. Latin text entitled, *D e revelatione inferni facta Guillelmo puero.*

THE VOYAGE OF ST. BRENDAN (NAVAGATIO SANCTI BRENDANI)

Although Brendan, an Irish saint, lived c. 486–577/83, the account of his voyage is from an early tenth-century narrative based on an eighth-century legend. The work is entitled *Navagatio Brendani*. It is a Latin prose work of the ninth century, perhaps as early as 800. The earliest surviving ms is from the tenth century. There is also a Latin verse *Navagatio* from c. 1100. The Latin prose *Navagatio* is sometimes conflated with the *Vita S. Brendani*. The Bollandists did not include a life of Brendan because they considered the whole story too fabulous. There is an Anglo-Norman verse version by Benedeit or Benoît (1121–1151), which dates from between 1106 and 1121. There is also an important Old Irish version, and the otherworld plays a much more prominent role in it than in the Latin version. There are also versions, dating mostly from the twelfth century, in English, Middle German, Low German, and Netherlandish.

This story differs considerably from the other works included in this volume, because it is not strictly a vision. The legend is based on what apparently are the true voyages of this saint who travelled as far as the Hebrides, Shetlands, Faroes, and Iceland; he may have travelled to the Azores, and some even think as far as Mexico. Brendan's soul does not leave his body, and he takes his journey to the otherworld in the company of seventeen companions who join him in his boat and set off in search of the Land of Promise of the Saints.

This type of work is called an *imrama*; but it has been included here because the influence of this work is so fundamental to the visions of the otherworld.

The critical literature on the *Voyage of Brendan* often focuses on it as a geographical map, but in the context in which it was written and in its context here it is more important as a spiritual map. A

51

great deal of attention is paid to the physical hardships endured by Brendan and his companions during their seven-year search for the Land of Promise of the Saints. One particular recurrent topic in this work is food: how it is obtained and prepared, and how often the travellers are required to fast because of short supplies of food. These are all details that point to the origins of this story among actual seafarers.

Brendan spends six years journeying, and during this time the Lord shows him the marvels of the ocean, which are described for us along with the wonders of the monastic and hermetic lifestyles that Brendan encounters on various islands.

He touches on the outskirts of hell, where he sees the forge of Vulcan and meets Judas Iscariot, who is enjoying a brief respite from his horrendous suffering. But all that Brendan sees occurs on the surface of the earth. Here he meets devils and saints and blessed souls enjoying eternal bliss in the Land of Promise of the Saints. He is told that this Land will be revealed when the "days of tribulation come upon the people of Christ."

It is important to note that, in imitation of the very physical dimension of this and other voyages, the line between vision and experience becomes blurred in many of the later visions of the otherworld. For instance, although Tundale clearly leaves his body behind when he "goes on" his vision, he nevertheless experiences the torments of hell as if his body were present along with his soul.

Bibliographical Works

140   BHL 1: 21–18; Supp. 59–60, New Supp. 16–65.

141   Bosner, W. *Anglo-Saxon and Celtic Bibliography, 1450–1807.* 2 vols. Berkeley: University of California Press, 1957, vol. 1, nos. 6238–82.

142   Lapidge, Michael, and Richard Sharpe. *A Bibliography of Celtic-Latin in Literature, 400–1200.* Dublin: Royal Irish Academy, 1985, no. 362, pp. 105–6.

143   Selmer, C., ed. *Navagatio Sancti Brendani Abbatis: From Early Latin.* Publications in Medieval Studies 16. Notre Dame, Ind.: University of Notre Dame Press, 1959; rpt. Dublin: Four Courts Press, 1989.

144   ———. "The Vernacular Translations of the Navagatio Sancti Brendani: A Bibliographical Study." *Medieval Studies* 18 (1956): 145–57.

Sources

145   Auracher, Theodor, ed. "Der Brandan der Arsenalhandschrift BLF 283." *Zeitschrift für Romanische Philologie* 2(1878): 438–57.

       Diplomatic edition of the Old French verse version of *Brendan's Voyage.*

146   Balz, Martha. *Die M.E. Brendanledende des Gloucester-legenders: Kritisch herausgegeben mit einleitung.* Berlin: Mayer & Müller, 1909.

       Introduction covers the manuscript tradition, sources, meter, and language. Presents a critical edition of the Middle English text.

147   Bartsch, Karl. "Saint Brendan." *La Langue et les littératures françaises depuis le ixe jusqu'au xie siécle.* Paris: Maisonneuve & C. Leclerc, 1887, vv. 69–83.

       Critical edition of Old French verse versions.

148   Bayerschmidt, Carl F., and Carl Selmer. "An Unpublished Low German Prose Version of the

Navagatio Sancti Brendani." *Germanic Review* 30 (1955): 83–91.

An edition of the text found on four unnumbered leaves of the *Legenda aurea* of the British Library (3851 ee 16), accompanied by information on sourcerenditionprovenance, scribe, and dialect.

149   Bellemans, A. T. W. *De reis van Sente Brandane, naar den Comburgschentekst.* Antwerp: Nederlandsche Boekhandel, 1942.

An edition of the Middle Dutch verse version with an introduction and bibliography.

150   Benz, Richard. *Sanct Brandans Meerfahrt.* Jena: Diederichs, 1927.

Not seen. Modernized edition of the Volksbuch.

151   Bergsma, Jan. *Bijgdrage tot de wordingsgeschiedenis en de critiek der Middelnederlandsche Branden-teksten.* Groningen: B. Wolters, 1887.

Not seen. Dutch language text.

152   Bonebakker, E. *Van sente Brandane naar het Comburgsche en het Huthemsche Handschrft, opniew uitgegeven.* Amsterdam: Binger, 1894.

Not seen.

153   Brill, W. G. "Van sinte Brandaen in Panthalioen, naar het utrechtsche Handschrift." *Bibliotheek van middelnederlandsche Letterkunde* 6 (1871): 1–77 (Groningen: 1871).

Not seen. A translation dating from the thirteenth or fourteenth century of a German rhymed version, now lost.

154   Bute, The Marquess of (John P. C. Stuart). "Brendan's Fabulous Voyage." *The Scottish Review* 21(Jan. and April 1893): 35, 73; rpt. "St. Brendan." *County Louth Archeological Society Journal* 2(1909): 109–23.

Synopsis of the *Voyage* with general introductory remarks as an annual address to the society. Supports idea of the voyage as imaginary rather than factual.

155   Calmund, Heinrich. *Prolegomena zu einer kritischen Ausgabe des ältesten französischen Brendanlebens.* Bonn: S. Foppen, 1902.

Not seen. *Vita.*

156   Dahlberg, Torsten, ed. *Brandaniana: Kritische Bemerkungen zu den Untersuchungen uber die deutschen und niederlandischen Brandan. Acta Universitatis Gothoburgensis* 64 (1958), part 5: 1–149.

An edition of the Middle Low German poem. Introduction discusses the tradition of the work, the mss and printed editions, and the relationship of the poem to other German versions. Includes bibliography.

157   Draak, Maartje. *De Reis van sinte Brandaan.* Amsterdam: Meulenhoff, 1949.

Combines text from Brill (**153**) with variants from earlier edition. Provides facing modern Dutch translation by Bertus Aafjes.

158   Fay, Rolf D. *Sankt Brandan: Zwei Fruhnerhochdeutsche Prosafassung.* Stuttgart: Helfant, 1985.

Critical edition based on edition by Anton Sorg (1476) and Gabriel Rollenhagens.

159   Gardiner, see **32**, pp. 81–127.

Includes an English translation of the *Navagatio* with notes and bibliography.

160   Geck, Elisabeth, ed. *Sankt Brandans Seefahrt. Faksililedruck d. Originalausg. Augsburg um 1476.* Wiesbaden: Pressler, 1969.

Not seen. Facsimile of incunabulum.

161   Gignani, Antonietta. *Navagatio Sancti Brendani, La navagazione di San Brandano.* Milan: P. unk., 1975.

Not seen.

162   Hamel, A. G. van. *Primitieve Ierse Taalstudie.* Amsterdam: Noord-Hollandsche, 1946.

Not seen. Old Irish.

163   Hilka, A. *Drei Erzählungen aus dem didaktischen Epos "L'Image du Monde" (Brandanus – Nature – Secundus).* Halle: M. Niemeyer, 1928, 1–49

Not seen.

164   Horstmann, Carl. *Early South English Legendary.* Early English Text Society 87. London: E.E.T.S., 1887, 220–40. Rpt. *Archiv für Studium der Neieren Sprachen und Lieratur* 53 (1874): 16–48.

Edition of metrical thirteenth century Middle English text. based on Laud 108, Harley 2277, Ashmol 43, Vernon 107, Lambeth 223 and Trinity College Cambr. R. 3, 25.

165   Jubinal, Achille. *La Légende latine de S. Brendaines avec une traducion inédite en prose et en poésie romanes.* Paris: Teuchner, 1836, 105–6.

An edition of the Provencal fragment of 1740 verses, introduced by Gautier de Metz in the second edition of his *Image du Monde.* Based on Paris B.N. Fr. 1444.

166   Marchand, see **97**, pp. ii–viii, xxiv–xxvi, 1–77.

Provides a brief introduction, bibliography, and French translation of the Anglo-Norman text of Benoît.

167   Martin, Ernst, ed. "Die Lateinische Ubersetzung der altfranzösischen Gedichts auf St. Brendan." *Zeitschrift für deutsches Altherthum* 16 (1873): 289–322.

Diplomatic edition of the thirteenth century metrical translation of the Anglo-Norman poem into Latin. B.L. Cotton Vesp. D. ix.

168   ———, ed. *La Vie de saint Brandan.* Paris: P. Unk., 1880.

Not seen

169 Meyer, Kuno. "Ein mittelirisches Gedicht den Meerfahrer." *Sitzungsberichte der kgl. Preuss. Akademie der Wissenschaften* 76 (1912): 436–43.

Not seen.

170 Meyer, Paul. "Legendes Hagiographiques en Français." *Histoire Litteraire de la France*. Paris: Imprimerie Nationale, 1906, 33: 341–42, 378–458.

Lists French octosyllabic verse versions by Benoît (c.1121) (mss: London, B.L. Cotton. Vesp. B.x; Oxford, Bodl. Rawlinson, misc. 1370; Paris B.N. Nouv. acq. fr. 4503 [formerly Ashburnham 112]; York, Chapter Library 16 K 12); and a thirteenth century version (Arsenal 3516) edited in *Zeitschrift für Romanische Philologie* (see **145**); and a version introduced by Gautier of Metz (see **165**). Description of prose versions dispersed throughout discussion on pp. 378–458.

171 Meyer, Wilhelm. "Die Uberlieferung der deutschen Brandanslegende" Ph.D. Diss.: University of Gottingen, 1918.

Discusses the prose Brendan legend, the mss, their relationships, reviewing previous research, and in an appendix examines the preservation in the prose text of rhyme words from the verse versions, and the depiction of the legend in the graphic arts.

172 Michel, Francisque, ed. *Les voyages merveilleux de Saint Brendan à la recherche du paradis terrestre. Legende en vers du xiie siècle, publié d'apres le*

manuscrit du Musée Britannique. Paris: A. Claudin, 1878.

Diplomatic edition of Anglo-Norman text based on London, B.L. Cotton Vesp. B. x., with an introduction covering earlier editions and the historic background of the legend, and providing a brief description of the narrative.

173   Moltzer, H. E., ed. "Levers en Legenden van heiligen Brandaen in Panthalioen, naar het utrechtsche Handschrift." *Bibliotheek van middelnederlandsche Letterkunde* (XVL). Leiden: Sijthoff; Groningen: Wolters, 1891.

Edition of Middle Dutch text with brief introduction.

174   Moran, Patrick F., ed. *Acta Sancti Brendani.* Dublin: William Bernard Kelly, 1872, 85–131.

Latin documents connected with the life of Brendan, including the prose and metrical *Vitae,* the *Oratio,* and the *Navagatio* (critical edition).

175   Muller, J. W. "Brandaris en Sint-Brandarius." *Nederl. Tidskr. en Letterk.* 16 (1895).

Not seen.

176   ———. "Nog iets over Sint-Brnadarius." *Nederl. Tidskr. en Letterk.* 18 (1897).

Not seen.

177 ———. "Sporen van Oudermansche en andere overleverindgen in middeleeuwsch-Nederlandsche Geschriften." *Nederl. Tidskr. en Letterk.* 30 (1911).

Not seen.

178 Novati, Francesco, ed. *La "Navagatio Sancti Brendani" in antico veneziano.* Bergamo: Istituto d'arti grafiche, 1892 and 1896; rpt. Bologna: Forni, 1973.

Edition of the Venetian (Italian) prose version based on a unique ms (Ambrosiana D. 158 inf.). Includes a ms description and extensive discussion of the language of the Venetian version. Discusses the major versions, the four Italian versions (all prose) and the ms; includes a literary introduction describing the narrative. Review by C. Boser, *Romania* 22 (1893): 578–90.

179 O'Donoghue, Denis, ed. and trans. *Brendaniana: St. Brendan the Voyager in Story and Legend.* Dublin: Browne & Nolan, 1893.

A collection of material in English relating to Brendan, including an account of the cathedral at Ardfert-Brendan; translations of the Irish "Life of Brendan"; the Latin *Navagatio* (pp. 111–75), and the Latin "Life"; Legends of Brendan; geographic lore regarding Irish settlements in North America before the tenth century; a description of a pilgrimage to Brandon Mountain (6/28/1868); appendix includes the Early English metrical life and the Early English prose life of Brendan.

180 O'Kelly, John Joseph. *Betha Bhréandain. A Imtrheachta is a iomrémha.* Dublin: M. H. Macguill, 1915.

Irish text. Includes bibliography.

181   O'Meara, John, trans. *The Voyage of Brendan: Journey to the Promised Land.* Atlantic Highlands, N.J.: Humanities Press, 1976.

Includes introduction. English text is a translation from Latin based on edition by Selmer (see **143**). Brief introduction treats the Brendan/America question and literary questions, such as the appeal of the narrative and its stylistic qualities of symmetry and repetition. Sees the work as a stylized, abstract, non-naturalistic narrative that shows sophistication and humor. Discusses his translation in the light of the need for one which is accessible.

182   Orlandi, Ioannes, ed. *Navagatio Sancti Brendani.* Testi e documenti per lo studio dell'antichità 38. Milan and Varese: Istituto Editoriale Cisalpino, 1968.

Discusses mss and redactions of Latin and Irish versions; the relationship between the *Vita* and the *Navagatio*, the relationship of the *Navagatio* to the *imrama* and to other visions of heaven and hell, and the date and place of composition. Includes bibliography. This volume was apparently designed as a first volume, with the second as an edition of the Latin text, but it is not clear that this second volume was ever published.

183   Oskamp, H. P. A., ed. *De reis van Sente Brandane, naar de versie in het Comburgsche handschrift.* Zutphen: P. unk., 1971.

Not seen.

184   Pfitzner, Erich. *Das anglonormannische Gedicht von Brandan als Quelle einer lateinischen Prosafassung.*

Halle: Karras, 1910; rpt. *Zeitschrift für Romanische Philologie* 35 (1911): 31–66.

Comparison of versions. Dissertation: Halle-Wittenburg.

185   Plummer, Charles. *Bethada Náem nErenn: Lives of Irish Saints.* Oxford: Clarendon Press, 1922, 1: 44–95, 2: 44–92.

Includes the prose *Life of Brendan* (1:44–95, 2:44–92), based on Brussels, B.R. 4190–200; and the verse *Twelve Apostles of Ireland* or Brendan II (1:98–102, 2:93–98), based on the Liber Flavus Fergusiorum (Dublin, Royal Irish Academy); London, B.L. Egerton 1781; and Brussels B.R. 2324–40 and 5100–4. Vol. 1 contains an introduction (xvi–xxv) discussing the relationship between the *vitae* and the *Navagatio* and editions of the Irish texts; vol. 2 contains English translations.

186   ———. *Vitae Sanctorum Hiberniae.* 2 vols. Oxford: Clarendon Press, 1910, 1: xxxvi–xliii, 98–151; 2: 270–94.

A Latin edition of the *Vita S. Brendani* that has the *Navagatio* (ch. 12–66) embedded in the text; a *Vita* that is actually a peculiar Latin recension of the *Navagatio*; plus curious satirical verses on the *Navagatio*. Introduction discusses the mss and the relationship of various Latin versions and the Anglo-Norman poem.

187   Riber, L. "Els camins del Paradis perdut." *Biblioteca Literària* 31 (1920): 2–189. Rpt. in L. Riber. *Obres completes.* Barcelona: P. unk., 1949, 1245–1319.

Not seen.

188 Ruhe, Ernstpeter, ed. *Le Voyage de Saint Brendan.* Klassische Texte des romanischen Mitterlaters in zweisprachisen Ausgaben 16. Munich: W. Fink, 1977.

Text in Old French with introduction and parallel translation in German. Includes bibliography and list of manuscripts.

189 Schröder, Karl. *Sanct Brandan: Eine lateinischer und drei deutsche Texte.* Erlangen: E. Besold, 1871.

Latin prose edition based on two manuscripts and the edition of Jubinal (**166**); three German editions: two in verse (Middle German, thirteenth century Berlin *Germ.* Oct. 56; and Middle Low German, fifteenth century, Wolfenbüttel, *Helmstädt* 1203); and one in prose based on several printed editions.

190 ———. "Zum Brandan." *Germania: Vierteljahrsschrift für Deutsche Altherthumskande* 16 (1871): 60–74.

Comparison of the texts of the Netherlandisch and the Low German poetic versions of the Brendan legend.

191 Selmer, see **143**.

Briefly discusses the historical Brendan, the nature of the literary text, the manuscripts – of which there are 120 of the Latin prose version; discusses fully the eighteen manuscripts that he uses for his text. Provides a Latin edition with extensive notes, appendices of Latin editions and Latin mss. Includes an extensive bibliography up to 1959 (pp. 117–32). Lengthy and substantive review by J.

Carney (*Medium Aevum* 32 (1963): 37–44) deals primarily with certain names, the date and relationship of the *NB* to other Irish voyage literature.

192   Sherwood, Margaret Merriam. "Le Voyage de Saint Brandan: An Anglo-Norman Poem of the Twelfth Century." Ph.D. Diss.: Columbia University, 1918.

Not seen. Includes introduction, notes, glossary and bibliography.

193   Short, Ian and Brian Merrilees, ed. *The Anglo-Norman Voyage of St. Brendan.* Manchester: Manchester University Press, 1979.

Benedeit's text in Anglo-Norman verse with introduction and notes in English. Includes bibliographical references and index. Includes list of Anglo-Norman manuscripts.

194   Steinweg, Carl. "Die handschriftlichen gestaltungen der lateinischen *Navagatio Brendani.*" *Romanische Forschungen* 7 (1893): 1–48.

A study of seventy-four mss to determine the relationships between them; also taking the Old French prose translation into consideration in constructing a hypothesis for the transmission of the text. Review by C. Boser in *Romania* 22 (1893): 578–90.

195   ———, ed. *Lives of Saints from the Book of Lismore.* Anecdota Oxeniensis, Mediaeval and Modern 5. Oxford: Clarendon, 1890, 99–116, 27–61.

Irish life of Brendan (99–116) with English translation (247–61).

196 Suchier, H., ed. *Brendans seefahrt. Romanische Studien.* Ed. by E. Böhmers. 1 (1875): 555–88.

Edition of Anglo-Norman text from B.L. Cotton Vesp. B.x., preceded by introduction discussing various versions of the work.

197 Thurneysen, Rudolf. "Eine Variante der Brendan Legende." *Zeitschrift für Celtische Philologie* 10 (1915): 408–20.

Twelve Apostles of Ireland (Life of Brendan II – verse) Critical edition of text based on Dublin, R.I.A., *Liber Fergusiorum* and other mss, with German translation.

198 Tuffrau, Paul. *Le merveilleux voyage de Saint Brandan à la recherche du Paradis.* Paris: L'Artisan du Livre, 1925.

Liberally using the Latin text published by Jubinal (**165**) and the two French texts in Jubinal (prose and verse), plus the French Michel text (**172**), Tuffrau "retells" the Brendan legend in contemporary French. No notes; general introduction.

199 Verwijs, Eelco. "Het Middelnederlandsche Gedicht van sinte Brandane." *Verslagen en Mededeelingen der K. Ak. van Wetensasch., Afd. Letterk., 2de reeks,* 2 (1872): 531–35.

Not seen.

200 ———. "Dr. Brill's uitgave van Sinte Brandaen." *De Taal- en Letterbode* 3 (1872): 235–56.

Comments of the text of Dr. Brill's edition, *Van Sinte Brandane* (**153**).

201   Villari, , see **72**: General, *Antiche Legende* 82–109, *Annali* 134–62.

Edition of Italian text based on Florence B.N. Cod. Magl. C.2. no. 1550.

202   Wahlund, Carl. *Brendans Seefahrt: Eine Altfranzosische prosaübersetzung aur dem xii/xii jahrhunderts nebst dem Lateinischen Original zum druck befordert.* Upsala: P. unk., 1891.

Not seen. Originally appeared in Latin with the title *Navagatio Brendani.*

203   ———. *Die Altfranzöische Prosaübersetzung von Brendans Meerfahrt nach der Pariser Handschrift Nat. Bibl. fr. 1553. Skrifter utgifna af K. Humanistiska Vetenskaps – Samfundet i Upsala 4, 3.* Upsala: Almquist & Wiskells, 1900.

Editions of a Old French prose versions from mss Paris B.N. 1553 and 1716; with, respectively, facing Latin texts based on ms. Paris B.N. 15076 and a composite text. Includes a glossary, bibliography, and a learned introduction on the life of Brendan, the Brendan legend, the mss of the Brendan legend (Latin, Old French, and a Norwegian/Icelandic fragment); the grammar of this edition; the relationship of the translation to the prototype; and the editions.

204   ———. "Eine alte provenzalische Prosaübersetzung von Brendans Meerfahrt." *Beiträge zur romanischen und*

englischen Philologie. Festgabe für Wendelin Förster. Halle: Niemeyer, 1902, 175–98.

Edition of shortened version of the thirteenth century Paris, Bibl. Nat. Fr. 9759 in High Languedoc.

205   Waters, E.G.R., ed. *The Anglo-Norman Voyage of St. Brendan by Benedeit: A Poem of the Early Twelfth Century.* Oxford: Clarendon, 1928; rpt. Geneva: P. unk., 1974 .

A critical edition of the Anglo-Norman poem, written about 1121 for Adeliza, queen of Henry I, by a monk calling himself Benedeit. The introduction covers mss, author, date, versification, classification of manuscripts, relationship of Anglo-Norman poem to the *Navagatio*; Latin prose and rhymed translations, the language of the author, the text. Notes, glossary, index of proper nouns, appendix on some Anglo-Norman forms. Latin text in footnotes. London, B.L. Cotton Vesp. B.x. collated with York, Dean and Chapter Library 16 K 12; Oxford, Bodleian Rawlinson D. 913; Paris B.N. nouv. acqu. Fr. 4503; and Arsenal 3516.

206   ———. *An Old Italian Version of the "Navagatio Sancti Brendani."* Publications of the Philological Society 10. London: H. Milford and Oxford: Oxford University Press, 1931.

Discusses the ms (Tours, B.M. 1008), the translation, the language of the text (spelling, phonology, morphology and syntax); presents an annotated edition of the Tuscan text. Includes glossary and index of proper names.

207   Webb, J. F., ed. *Lives of the Saints.* Baltimore, Md.:
       Penguin, 1965, pp. 33–68; rpt. in D.H. Farmer, ed.,
       The Age of Bede. Baltimore: Penguin, 1983.

       A "plain, readable" translation of the *Voyage of St.
       Brendan* based on the edition of the Latin text by Carl
       Selmer. Also included in this volume is Bede's *Life of
       Cuthbert* and Eddius Stephanus' *Life of Wilfrid.*
       Introduction concentrates on the ecclesiastical history of
       Ireland. Brief introduction to *Voyage of Brendan* (pp. 18–
       20).

208   Wien, Max. *Das Verhältnis der handschriften anglo-
       normannischen Brandanlegende.* Halle: P. unk.,
       1886.

       Not seen. Old French.

209   Wright, Thomas, ed. *St. Brendan: A Medieval Legend of
       the Sea.* London: Percey Society, 1844; rpt. as *The
       Lyfe of Saynt Brandon,* London, 1844.

       Diplomatic edition of the Early English verse and
       prose Lives of St. Brendan from London, B.L. Harley
       2277.

Studies
210   Ancona, see **3**, pp. 48–53.

       Treats the antecedents of Dante in general and gives
       some particular attention to the Paul, Brendan, Tundale,
       Patrick, and Alberic visions. He does not make firm
       connections between these and the *Divine Comedy,* but
       indicates a general milieu of vision literature, which does
       not detract from Dante's originality.

211   Ashe, Geoffrey. *Land to the West: St. Brendan's Voyage to America.* London: Collins, New York: Viking, 1962.

     Speculates as extensively as possible on the geographic aspect of St. Brendan's voyage across the Atlantic, but concludes that the legend is a gigantic extension of an actual sea pilgrimage by Brendan in the Hebrides. Bibliography on exploration.

212   Babcock, William H. "The So-called Mythical Islands of the Atlantic in Medieval Maps: Considered as Evidence of Pre-Columbian Exploration Toward America." *Scottish Geographical Magazine* 31(May-August 1915): 261–69, 315–20, 360–71, 411–22.

     The geographical lore of early exploration; Brendan's voyage dealt with at 411–22.

213   ———. "St. Brendan's Explorations and Islands." *Geographical Review* 8 (1919): 37–46.

     Attempt to identify the islands of Brendan's voyage.

214   ———. *American Geographical Society of New York* Research Series 8(1922):31–38.

     Not seen.

215   Backer, Louis de. "La Légende flamande de S. Brandane sa bibliographie." Ed. by Edouard Rouveyre and Oct. Uzanne. *Miscellanées bibliographiques.* Paris: E. Rouveyre, 1878, 1:191–200.

     Brief discussion with bibliography.

216   Baer, C. H. "Des Heiligen Brendan Kapelle und Legende
       in Basel." *Basler Jahrbuch* 1939: 31–62.

       Peripherally discusses the voyages of Brendan.

217   Baum, Paul F. "Judas' Sunday Rest." *Modern Language
       Review* 18 (1923): 168–82.

       Discussion of Christian attitude toward Judas as
       revealed in the *NB* and of the oriental idea of Sunday rest
       introduced into Western literature.

218   Bayot, Alphonse. "Le Voyage de saint Brendan dans les
       légendiers français: essai de classement dans
       manuscrits." *Melanges d'Histoire offerts à Charles
       Moeller* 1. Louvain: Catholic University, 1914, 1:
       456–67.

       Classification of twenty mss.

219   Beckers, Hartmut. "Brandan und Herzog Ernst. Eine
       Untersuchung ihres Verhältnis anhand der
       Morivparallelen." *Leuvense Bijdragen* 59:1 (1970):
       41–55.

       Not seen.

220   Bejczy, István. "Brandaan ende antipoden." *Millenium*
       2.1 (1988): 1–8.

       Not seen.

221   Bernier, Gildas. "Les navires celtiques du Haut Moyen
       Age." *Etudes Celtiques* 16 (1979): 287–91.

Brief article on ships and navigation among the Celts drawing on the Brendan legend for evidence.

222　Bieler, Ludwig. "Casconius, the Monster of the *Navagatio Brendani.*" *Eigse* 5 (1947): 139–40.

Discusses the monster's name: Iasconius in the *Navagatio* and Casconius in the *Vita* in the Rawlinson manuscript.

223　———. "Two Observations Concerning the *Navagatio S. Brendani.*" *Celtica* 11 (1976): 15–17.

Briefly discusses two points: the first concerning the relationships between the *NB* and the *Voyage of Máel Dúin,* and the second on the identification of several particular islands mentioned in the *NB.*

224　Birkenhof, Richard. *Ueber metrum und reim der altfranzösischen Brandanlegende.* Ausgaben und abhandlungen aud dem gebiete der romanischen philologie 19. Marburg: Elwert, 1884; rpt. *Ausgaben und Abhandlungen aus dem Gebiete der Romanischen Philologie* 19 (1884): 1–95.

Study of the poetics of the Old French version of the *NB.*

225　Bouet, Pierre. *La fantastique dans la litterature latine du Moyen Age: La navagation de saint Brendan.* Caen: Centre d'etudes et de la recherches pour l'antiquite, 1986.

Contains introduction, bibliography and illustrations accompanying extracts from the anonymous Latin text with facing modern French text, a simplified Latin text, and the corresponding text by Benedeit with a modern French translation of Benedeit, all annotated.

226   Boas, George **(9)** , pp. 154–74.

Study of "primitivism" which examines the idea of the earthly paradise using several examples but in particular the *Vision of Tundale, St. Patrick's Purgatory,* and *St. Brendan's Voyage.*

227   Brekke, K. *Etude sur la flexion dans Le Voyage de S. Brandan. Poème anglo-normand du xiie siècle.* Paris: F. Vieweg, 1884.

Not seen. Philological or textual comment on OF verse Voyage.

228   Brown, A.C.L. "Barintus." *Revue celtique* 22 (1901): 339–44.

An examination of Barintus, a character in both the *Navagatio* and the *Vita Merlini.* The author concludes that Barintus seems to be a survival of some Celtic sea god who mysteriously and probably independently appeared in both these works.

229   ——. "The Wonderful Flower that Came to St. Brendan." In *Manly Anniversary Studies in Language and Literature.* Chicago: University of Chicago Press, 1923, 295–99; rpt. Freeport, N.Y.: Books for Libraries, 1968.

Essay on rare prologue concerning a flower that occurs in Irish text of the *Voyage* **(197)** and the antecedents for this prologue in ancient Irish literature.

230   Burrell, Margaret. "Narrative Structures in 'Le Voyage de St. Brendan.'" *Parergon* 17 (1977): 3–9.

Delineates two main quest structures which form a "type of interlace pattern which at the same time unifies and diversifies the complexities of the structural pattern."

231   Carp, Teresa. "The Three Late-Coming Monks: Tradition and Invention in the *Navagatio Sancti Brendani.*" *Medievalia et Humanistica* n.s. 12 (1984): 127–42.

Through the layering of narrative the story of the latecomers mirrors and foreshadows the narrative progress of the frame tale — the larger story of death and rebirth. Claims that the narrative manipulation reveals a sophistication that is remarkable for the time.

232   Caulkins, Janet Hillier. "Les notations numériques et temporelles dans la *Navagation de saint Brendan* de Benedeit." *Le Moyen Age* 80 (1974): 25–60.

Not seen.

233   Chapman, Paul H. *The Man who Led Columbus to America.* Atlanta: Judson, 1973.

Brendan as possible precursor to Columbus.

234   Dahlberg, Torsten. "Der hochdeutsche Zweig der Brendanüberlieferung." *Suomalaisen Tiedeakateian Toimituksia (Annales Academiae Scientiarum Fennicae),* ser. B 8 (1954): 53–66.

Not seen.

235   Daly, Dominick. "The Legend of St. Brendan." *Celtic Review* 1(1905): 135–47.

Discusses the legend of the voyage claiming that Brendan himself had correct information about the West Indian Islands and the continent beyond and apparently made some attempt to cross the Atlantic, but was unsuccessful and was not "converting pagans" there.

236   De Goeje, J. *"La légende de Saint Brendan."* Actes du 8e Congrès International des Orientalistes, 1889, Stockholm and Christiania. Leiden: P. unk., 1893, 3–76.

Not seen.

237   ———. *Brandaan en Virgilius.* Amsterdam: Meulenhoff, 1957.

Text of talk, with bibliographical references included, making comparisons between the cosmologies of Virgil and the Brendan legend.

238   ———. "Rekenschap na vijf-en-twintig jaar." *Leuvense Bijdragen* 59:1 (1970): 82–92.

Not seen. Stocktaking after 25 years.

239   Djurhuus, Hans A. *Sankta Brandan.* Tórshavn: P. Unk., 1936.

Not seen.

240   Dunn, Joseph. "The Brendan Problem." *Catholic Historical Review* 6 (1920–21): 395–477.

Survey of research to 1921 with select bibliography.

241 Dumville, David N. "Two Approaches to the Dating of the *Navagatio Sancti Brendani.*" *Studi medievali* 29:1 (1988): 87–102; also in *Romano barbarica* 8 (1983).

Not seen.

242 Edel, Doris. "Antipoden, ankers en een wereld-onder-het-water." In *Tussentijds: Bundel studies aangebogen aan W.P. Gerristenn ter gelegenheid van zijn vijftigste Verjaardag.* Ed. by A.M.J. van Buuren. Utrecht: HES Uitgevers, 1985. 101–14, 339–42.

Discusses the possible influence of Irish literature on the Middle Dutch *Reis van Sinte Brandaan.*

243 Esposito, Mario. "Un fragment de la *Navagatio Sancti Brendani* en ancien Venetien." *Mélanges philologiques* 5(1921): 22ff.

Not seen.

244 ———. "Sur la Navagatio sancti Brendani et sur les versions italiennes de la Navagatio." *Romania* 64 (1938): 328–46.

Includes a list and description of 99 mss, notes on the authorship and diffusion of the *Navagatio,* and on its popularity as a pseudo-geographical text.

245 ———. "An Apocryphal 'Book of Enoch and Elias' as a Possible Source of the *Navagatio Sancti Brendani.*" *Celtica* 5 (1960): 192–206.

Discusses the *NSB* as a book of fantasy with a possible source in apocryphal literature.

246   Evans, S. "Judas Iscariot's Paradise." *Brother Fabian's Manuscript.* London and Cambridge: P. unk., 1885.

Not seen.

247   Fleuriot, Léon. "Les récite de navagation." In *Histoire Litteraire et culturelle de la Bretagne: Heritage celtique et captation francaise des origines à la fin des Etats.*" Ed. by Leon Fleuriot and Auguste-Pierre Ségalen. Paris and Geneva: Champion-Slatkine, 1987.

Discusses the journeys of St. Malo, St. Brendan, and the Breton sailors who discovered relics of St. Matthew.

248   Gerritsen, W.P. "Zeilen met sint Brandaan." *Spiegel Historiael* 15:3 (1980): 171–80.

On geographical lore.

249   Hammer, Wilhelm. *Die sprache der anglonorman-nischen Brandanslegende.* Halle: aP. unk., 1885; rpt. *Zeitschrift für Romanische Philologie* 9 (1885): 75–115.

Brief discussion of manuscripts followed by extensive, philological comment on Old French *Navagatio.*

250   Hanning, Robert W. "Mony turned tyme: the Cycle of the Year as a Religious Symbol in Two Medieval Texts." In *Saints, Scholars and Heros.* Ed. by Margot King

and Wesley Stevens. Collegeville, Minn.: Hill
Monastic Library, 1979, 1:281–98.

Discusses circular motion as an image of perfection
and stasis in the *Navagatio.*

251 Hennig, John. "A Note on Ireland's Place in the Literary
     Tradition of St. Brendan." *Traditio* 8 (1952): 397–
     402.

     Discusses the Irish tradition of Brendan's *Voyage* as
     opposed to the continental tradition and makes a case for
     the influence of this tradition on medieval literature.
     Reviews recent scholarship.

252 Hogetoorn, Corry. "Le *Voyage de Saint Brandan* par
     Benedeit." *Rapports: Het Fanse Boek* 55:3 (1985):
     110–24.

     Discusses the historic person, the texts associated
     with the legend, the relationship of the text to hagiography
     and *imrama*; provides a synopsis of the poem and a
     bibliography.

253 Hull, Eleanor. "The Legend of St. Brendan." *The New
     Irish Review* 4 (1916): pp. unk.

     Not seen.

254 Illingworth, R.N. "The Structure of the Anglo-Norman
     Voyage of St. Brendan by Benedeit." *Medium Aevum*
     55 (1986): 217–29.

     Examines the structure of this work to show that it is
     a "masterpiece of organization, whose constituent parts
     are created by parallels and contrasts of theme and style

(frequently involving the use of key-words) and that far from being a sequence of episodes loosely cobbled together around a central theme, the poem has a grand design based on a nine-fold cruciform pattern."

255   Ireland, John de Courcy and David C. Sheehy, eds. *Atlantic Visions.* Dublin: Boole, 1989.

Proceeding of the first International Conference of the Society of Saint Brendan. Sept. 1985. Essays generally on discovery and exploraton, except for articles by MacCana (**270**), O Caoimh (**274**), and Lemarchand (**267**)

256   Jones, Robin F. "The Mechanics of Meaning in the Anglo-Norman 'Voyage of Saint Brendan.'" *Romanic Review* 71:2 (1980): 105–13.

Discusses narrative structure to find a work unified more by contrast than by consequence.

257   Kenney, James. (see **90**), pp. 406–17.

Discusses the *Navagatio* in relationship to the *Vita,* with descriptions of additional Brendan-related material. Excellent bibliography up to 1929. Identifies six versions of the *NB* and lists mss for each version.

258   ———. "The Legend of St. Brendan." *Transactions of the Royal Society of Canada,* ser. 3.14, sect. 2 (1920): 51–67.

Discusses the historical Brendan, the historical background of the legend, the versions of the legend, and the background in literature and folklore.

259   ———. "The Legend of St. Brendan." *Revue Celtique* 39
         (1922): 393–95.

         Brief bibliographic essay.

260   Kervran, Louis. *Brandan, le Grand Navigateur Celte du
         vi^e siecle.* Paris: Laffont, 1977.

         Basically a discussion of the geographical reality of
         the voyages with an examination of the texts relating to
         the voyage.

261   Klerk-Oppenhuis De Jong, S. I. "Brandaan en het geloof
         in Gods genade. Structur analuyse van het
         Middlenederlandse gedicht van Sente Brandane."
         Tijdschrift vor Nederlandse taal-en leetterkunds 105:
         4 (1989): 21–51.

         Not seen. Brendan and belief in God's mercy.
         Structural analysis of the Middle Dutch poem of St
         Brendan.

262   Kölbing, Eugen. "Christian von Troyes, Yvain und die
         Brandanuslegende." *Zeitschrift für vergleichende
         Literaturgeschichte* n.f. 11–12 (1897–98): 442–48.

         Briefly discusses certain motifs common to the two
         works, mainly the tree full of birds.

263   Krenn, Ernst. "Wer hat Amerika zuerst entdeckt?"
         Petermanns geographische Mitteilungen 95 (1950):
         207–11.

         On the geographical veracity of the voyage.

264   Langlois, Louis. *La découverte de l'Amérique par les Normands vers l'an 1000. Deux sagas islandaises.* Paris: Société d'éditions géographiques, maritimes et coloniales, 1924.

Not seen. Voyage of Brendan discussed pp. 107–10.

265   Larmat, Jean. "L'eau dans la *Navagation de Saint Brandan* de Benedeit." *Senefiance* 15 (1985): 233–46.

Not seen.

266   Lavery, Simon. "The Source of the St. Brendan Story in the South English Legendary." *Leeds Studies in English* n.s. 15 (1984): 21–32.

Considers the Latin *NSB* to be the direct source for the *South English Legendary* not drawing from the Anglo-Norman poem by Benedeit.

267   Lemarchand, M. I. "'Li Salt Brandan': Navigation and Flight, a Contribution to the Study of the Fantastic Narrative in Benedeit's 'Voyage of St. Brendan.'" (See **255.**)

Examines the symbolic meaning underlying the saint's departure as told by Benedeit.

268   Little, George A. *Brendan, the Navigator.* Dublin: Gill, 1945.

On Brendan's life and voyages with particular attention to the role of Brendan in the opening of the western hemisphere.

269   Low, C. E. *Description and Classification of the Manuscripts of the* Navagatio Sancti Brendani. Abstracts. Oxford: P. unk., 1935.

Not seen.

270   MacCana, Pronsais. "The Voyage of St. Brendan: Literary and Historical Origins." See **255**, pp. 3–16.

Examines historical and literary precedents to explain how such a text as the *Navagatio* came to be written in the ninth century and why it possessed such a strong cultural influence.

271   Merkle, Sebastian. "Die Sabbathruhe in der Hölle." *Romanische Quartalschrift* 9 (1895): 484–509.

Not seen.

272   Merrilees, Brian. "The Anglo-Norman Voyage of St. Brendan: Precocious or Unique? A Commentary on Recent Work." *Parergon* 31 (1981): 21–28.

Attempt to reevaluate the voyage as an innovative text, at the same time recognizing it as a singular work of saint's adventure.

273   Mulder, Maaike. "De filiatie van de Reise/Reis-Teksten van de Brandaan." *Tijdschrift voor Nederlandse taal-en leetterkunds* 105: 2–3 (1989): 132–51.

Not seen. The filiation of the Reise/Reis texts of Brandaan., includes texts and illustrations.

274   O Caoimh, Tomás. "St. Brendan Sources: St. Brendan and Early Irish Hagiography." See **255**, 17–42.

A study of hagiographical material.

275   Oskamp, H. P. A. *The Voyage of Máel Dúin*. Groningen:
       P. unk., 1970.

       Not seen. Introduction discusses Brendan and
       imrama.

276   Palgen, Rudolf. *Brandansage und Purgatorio*.
       Heidelberg: P. unk., 1934.

       Not seen.

277   Peeters, L. "Brandanprobleme." *Leuvense Bijdragen* 59:1
       (1970): 3–27.

       Not seen.

278   ———. "De Reis van Sente Brandane, v. 137–260."
       Leuvense Bijdragen 59:1 (1970): 28–40.

       Not seen.

279   ———. "Das Quellenstudium der Navagtio Sancti
       Brendani, der mitteldeutschen und mittelnieder-
       landischen Brandenversion." *Leuvense Bijdragen*
       77:4 (1988): 411–34.

       Not seen.

280   Peters, Robert. "Die Reime der mittelniederländuschen
       Brandaen-Versionen." *Leuvense Bijdragen* 59:1
       (1970): 67–81.

       Not seen.

281   Plummer, Charles. "Some New Light on the Brendan
        Legend." *Zeitschrift für Celtische Philologie* 5
        (1905): 124–41.

        Study of the texts of Bodleian Rawlinson B 485 and
        505 containing a *Vita Brendani* that has been conflated
        with the *Navagation Brendani.*

282   Rekdal, Jan-Erik. "Med lukten av himmel i klaerne.
        Navagatio sankti Brendani og dens plass i irsk
        literatur." *Middelanderforum-Forum mediaevale* 8
        (1984): 5–35.

        Not seen. "With a smell on heaven in the clothes."
        Navagatio Sancti Brendani and its place in Irish literature.

283   Renan, Ernest. "La poésie des races celtiques." *Revue des
        Deux Mondes,* 1 Feb. 1854, pp. 500–6.

        Briefly discusses *NB* as the most exceptional
        example of the joining of Celtic naturalism and Christian
        Spiritualism. Reprinted in various editions of Renan's
        Essais de Morale et de Critique.

284   Ritchie, R.L.G. "The Date of the Voyage of St. Brendan."
        Medium Aevum 19 (1950): 64–66.

        Dates the Anglo-Norman *Voyage* by Benedeit to
        before 1 May 1118, possibly c. 1106.

285   Röcke,Werner. "Die Wahrheit der Wunder. Abenteuer
        der Erfahrung und des Erzählens im 'Brandan'- und
        'Apollonius'-Roman." In *Wege in die Neuzeit.* Ed.
        by Thomas Cramer. Forschungen zur Geschichte der
        alteren deutschen Literatur 8. Munich: Wilhelm Kink,
        1988, 252–69.

Examines the nature of the fantastic in the Brendan voyage and its relationship to "Apollonius von Tyrlant."

286   Runeberg, J. "Le Comte de l'Ile-Poisson." *Mémoires de la Societé Néophilologique à Helingfors* 3 (1902): 433ff.

Not seen.

287   Schirmer, G. "Zur Brendanus-Legende." Diss.: University of Leipzig, 1888.

Not seen.

288   Schulze, Alfred. "Zur Brendanlegende." *Zeitschrifte für Romanische Philologie* 30 (1906): 257–79.

Discusses the development of the Brendan Legend in connection with the life of Brendan and the feast of Easter.

289   ———. "Textkritisches zum altfranzosischen Prosa-Brendan. *Zeitschrifte für Romanische Philologie* 31 (1907): 188–99.

Bibliographical notes.

290   Schreiber, Georg. *Ireland im deutschen und abendländischen Sakralraum. Zugleich ein Ausblick auf St. Brandan und die zweite Kolumbus reise. Arbeitsgemeinschaft für Forschung des Landes Norgrhain-Westfalen Geistes wissenschaften* 19. Cologne: Westdeutcher Verlag, 1956.

Study of Brendan's voyage in the context of Irish missionary impetus.

291   Selmer, Carl "The Brendan Legend in Old German
       Literature." *Journal of the American Irish Historical
       Society* 32 (1941): 161–69.

       Brief article outlining the German version of the
       legend and providing an introduction to the geographical
       and spiritual nature of the text.

292   ———. "The Beginnings of the St. Brendan Legend on
       the Continent." *Catholic Historical Review* 29
       (1943): 169–76.

       Examines the spread of the legend to the continent
       through the possible intermediary of early monastic
       settlements on Britain and England and their manuscripts.

293   ———. "The Irish St. Brendan Legend in Lower
       Germany and on the Baltic Coast." *Traditio* 4 (1946):
       408–13.

       Traces an unexpected popularity and examines the
       importance of the Brethren of the Common Life in the
       transmission of this text into Lower Germany.

294   ———. "The Origin of Brandenburg (Prussia), the St.
       Brendan Legend, and the *Scoti* of the Tenth Century."
       Traditio 7 (1949–51): 16–33.

       Examines the role of the Scots in spreading the
       insular legendary material on the continent during their
       mission to the Slavs.

295   ———. "St. Brendan, the Navigator, in an Old German
       Cisiojanus of the 15th century." *Symposium* 37 [or
       38] (1984): 408–11.

Not seen.

296   ———. "A Study of the Latin Manuscripts of the
       Navagatio Sancti Brendani." *Scriptorium* 3 (1949):
       177–82.

       A brief study of the chronological and geographical
       distribution of manuscripts under various labels
       (*Navagatio, Vita, Liber, Visio,* etc.).

297   ———. "An Unknownm Manuscript of the *Navagatio
       Sancti Brendani* in U. S. A." *Scriptorium* 4 (1951):
       100–103.

       A note on and description of Brookland, Maryland,
       Franciscan College Library, Ms. 79 (Di Ricci
       1(1935):483).

298   ———. "Die Herkunft und Frühgeschiscte der *Navagatio
       S. Brendani.*" *Studien und Mitteilungen zur
       Geschichte des Benediktiner-ordens und seine
       Zweige* 67 (1956): 5–17.

       Not seen.

299   ———. "The Vernacular Translations of the Navagatio
       Sancti Brendani: A Bibliographical Study." *Medieval
       Studies* 18 (1956): 145–57.

       The proliferation of vernacular translations in the late
       Middle Ages resulted from a variety of "secular
       purposes, such as satisfying the curiosity of burghers and
       instructing seafarers, adventurers, cartographers and
       economists." Selmer discusses specifically translations
       into Germanic, Romance, and Celtic languages with an
       extensive bibliography on editions.

300 ———. "The Lisbon "Vita Sancti Brandani Abbatis." A hitherto Unknown *Navagatio*-text and Translation from Old French into Latin." *Traditio* 13 (1957): 313–44

Not seen.

301 Tardiola, Giuseppe. "I volgarizzamenti italiani della *Navagatio Sancti Brendani.*" *Rassegna della letteratura italiana* ser. 8, 90.3 (1986): 516–36.

Discusses the transformation of the *Navagatio* throughout the Italian translations.

302 Thrall, William F. "Clerical Sea Pilgrimages and the Imrama." In *The Manly Anniversary Studies in Language and Literature.* Chicago: University of Chicago Press, 1925, 276–83; rpt. Freeport, N.Y.: Books for Libraries, 1968.

Proposes that it is more likely that pagan elements were added to rich religious legends of adventurous pilgrimages made by sixth-century Irish clerics than the Christian elements were grafted onto pagan literature.

303 Vitaletti, Guido. "Curiosita e appunti: Una propaggini orale della leggendae di S. Brandano." *Miscellanea Studi.* Vol. 2, no. 42. Vatican Library, Rome.

Brief article on the oral tradition of the Brendan legend in Italy.

304 Walburg, E. "Sur le nom de l'auteur de Voyage de Saint Brendan." *Studia neophililogica* 12 (1939): 6–55.

Examines the authorship of the Anglo-Norman voyage attributed to Benedeit l'Apostoile.

305   Walsh, Honor. "Did St. Brendan Discover Brazil?" *American Catholic Historical Society of Philadelphia. Records* 38 (1927): 377–84.

More details for the dicscussion of Brendan in America.

306   Ward, H. L. D. *Catalog of Romances in the Department of Manuscripts in the British Museum.* London: British Museum, 1883–93, 2 (1893): 516–57.

Descriptions of Latin mss: Harley 3958, Cotton Vesp. A. xiv, Cotton Tiberius D. iii, Royal 8 E. xvii, Harley 3776; French mss: Cotton Vesp. B. x., Harley 108, Add. 15,106, Add. 6047, Cotton Tiberius E. i. Part i., Arundel 330, Cotton Vesp. D. ix, Cotton Vesp. B. x, Harley 4333, Add. 6524, Add. 17,275; English mss: Harley 2277, Add. 10,301, Cotton Julius D. ix, Add. 11,565.

307   Wilkie, James. *St. Brendan, the Voyager and his Mystic Quest.* London: Society of St. Peter and Paul, 1916.

Not seen.

308   Williamson, M. M. "The Dream of Cahus in *Perlesvaus.*" *Modern Philology* 3.1 (1932): 5–11. Rpt. as *Some Observations on the Legends of St. Brendan: A Comparison of an Episode in the* Navagatio *with one in* Perlesvaus *and the* Voyage of Maelduin. Chicago: Pvt. Prtd., 1933.

Discusses the incident of the theft by, and the resulting death of, one of Brendan's companions – an incident that also appears in the eighth-century *Voyage of Máel Dúin* and in the thirteenth-century *Perlesvaus*. The author of *Perlesvaus* apparently remembered the Celtic story but failed to understand it.

309   Winkelmann, J. H. "Prolog en expositie can de Middelnederlandse Brendaan." *Leuvense Bijdragen* 77.4 (1988): 411–34.

Not seen.

310   Yoder, Emily K. "The Monks' Paradise on The Land of Cokayne and the *Navagatio Sancti Brendani*." *Papers on Language and Literature* 19.3 (1983): 227–38.

Discusses similarities of these two works concluding that the author of the *Land of Cokayne* took advantage of the great popularity of the Brendan legend to write a parody of it with the main purpose of satirizing contemporary abuses of religious life and ridiculing contemporary geographical notions.

311   Zimmer, H. "Keltische Beiträge. Brendans Meerfahrt." *Zeitschrift für Deutsches Alterthum* 33 (1889): 129–220, 257–338.

Study of Brendan's voyage in Middle Irish literature, Brendan's voyage in the light of Irish *imrama*, and the promised land in the light of the Irish saga.

THE VISION OF CHARLES THE FAT (VISIO KAROLI TERTII/CRASSI)

This vision apparently occurred in 885. It is recorded, in about 1500 words, in the *Gesta regum anglorum* of William of Malmesbury who lived c. 1095–1143, and is based on Hariulf's *Chronicle*, Bk. 3, ch. 21. There was a wide interest in this text. Twenty mss survive, and reference to it is also made in the *Chronicle* of Helinand and in Vincent of Beauvais.

This is a very interesting and unusual vision. The visionary is Charles I, King of Swabia and Holy Roman Emperor. While Charles is resting on his bed a guide comes and leads him through his vision. The guide holds a ball of thread of great brightness made of light – a feature unique to this vision. The guide ties it around Charles' finger, and it not only casts light for their journey, but protects Charles from devils and provides a way by which the guide can lead Charles along. Charles is not punished during his vision.

Other major features of this work are also different from other visions. First of all, the visionary is a noble and a very powerful one. His vision, unlike the others, has a political agenda, which is not entirely unrelated to the important religious and ethical principle of nonviolence. In the infernal regions Charles meets only acquaintances like the bishops, vassals, princes, and counselors of his father and uncles, as well as his father, uncle, and cousin. All are being or have been punished for either counseling for, or partaking in, war.

This vision is also highly political. When Charles returns he announces that he has learned in his vision that he will be succeeded by his cousin and that he should give him the throne without opposition. In fact, his rule does end when his cousin Arnulf gains power after Charles makes a pact with the Vikings, offering them Normandy in return for their sparing Paris. Such prophesy after the fact is a device used by Dante with disarming effect.

The geography of the otherworld is not very clearly distinguished; everything appears to take place on one plain through which Charles passes from those undergoing the worst punishments to those who have already passed beyond punishment. This vision encourages the living to aid the dead through Masses, prayers, psalms, alms, and vigils, invoking the aid provided to the dead by the saints, particularly here St. Peter and St. Remigius.

Sources

312   Gardiner, see **32**, pp. 129–33.

        Includes English translation of vision with notes and bibliography.

313   Hariulf. *Chronicon Centulense ou Chronique de l'Abbeye de Saint-Riquier.* Ed. by Ernest Prarond. Trans. by the Marquis Le Ver. Mémoires de la Société d' Émulation d'Abbeville. Abbeville: Fourdrinier, 1899, 153–58.

        French translation with a few notations and no real introduction.

314   ——. "Die Vision Kaiser Karls III." *Neues Archiv der Gesellschaft für altere deutsche Geschichtskunde* 27 (1902): 399–08, 493–502.

        Not seen.

315   ——. *Chronique de l'Abbaye de Saint-Riquier.* Ed. by Ferdinand Lot. Paris: Picard, 1894, 144–50.

Introduction on the life and works of the author, as well as a discussion of the *Chronicon Centulense,* its sources and influences, the transmission of the text and the basis for this Latin edition.

316   PL 174:1287–91.

Edition of Hariulf, *Chronicon Centulense,* reprinted from the *Spicilegium Dachery.*

317   William of Malmesbury. *De Gestis Regum Anglorum Libri Quinque, Historiae Nouellae Libri Tres.* Ed. by William Stubbs. Rolls Series 90. London: Public Record Office, 1807, 1:112–16.

Annotated critical edition of Latin text.

318   ———. *History of the Kings of England.* Edited by John Sharpe. London: Longman, Hurst, Rees, Orme & Brown: 1815, 117–21.

English translation of *Gesta regum* based on printed sources and mss, esp. London. B.L. Reg. 13, D. II. The vision appears in Bk. 2, ch. 2 (CE 855).

319   ———. *Chronicle of the Kings of England.* Ed. by J. A. Giles. London: Bohn, 1847, 102–5.

English translation based on London, B.L. Reg. 13, D. II. Introduction discusses William, his writings, his style, and the early editions of his *Chronicle.*

Studies
320   Levison, see **47**.

Study of political aspects of early medieval vision literature with particular attention to the visions of Charles the Fat and Bernoldus.

321   Poupardin, René. "La date de la Visio Karoli tertii." *Bibliothèque de l'Ecole des chartes* 64 (1903): 284–88.

Dates the *Vision of Charles the Fat* to shortly after Charles' death, placing it in or around the diocese of Rheims.

322   Silverstein, Theoodore. "'Inferno' XII 100–126 and the 'Visio Caroli Crassi." *Modern Language Notes* 51 (1936): 9–52.

Remarks on Dante's precedent of the *Vision of Charles the Fat* for the punishment of those who out of greed for earthly things are guilty of bloodshed and rapine.

THE VISION OF CHRISTINA MIRABILIS

This vision of heaven and purgatory appears in the biography, (Ch. 1, bk. 6–7, *Vita Beatae Christinae Mirabilis Trudonopoli in Hasbania* by Thomas de Cantimpré. Christina, who lived from 1150–1224 in Brabant-Flanders, had a truly amazing life, especially after her apparent death when this vision occurred.

During her vision she saw many people who were known to her in the flesh. She describes the pains of purgatory as "so cruel that no tongue can tell of them." In heaven she meets the Lord who asks her to return to earth and endure suffering to help deliver those in purgatory, a challenge that she accepts and returns to a life that takes on the aura of a fable.

Sources
323   AS July 5, pp. 637–60.

Edition of Latin *Vita* edited by J. Pinius.

324   Petroff, see **60**, pp. 184–85.

English translation of vision preceded by brief introduction on Christina in the context of feminine spirituality (175–76).

THE VISION OF DRYTHELM

This vision is included for the date 699 CE in the *Chronicle* of Roger of Wendover, and according to Vincent of Beauvais' (d. 1264) *Vision of an English Man* it occurred in 941. Bede, however, lists it under 696 CE in his *Historia Ecclesiastica Gentis Anglorum* (Bk. 5, ch. 12), in about 1600 words, which was written in 731 in England in Latin. Bede's text is derived from the *relatio* of Haemgisl.

Drythelm was a good man from Northumbria who became sick and appeared to die, but his soul was led to the otherworld by an anonymous guide with a shining countenance, wearing a bright garment. A limited number of sins are treated here, although both fire and ice are used as punishment. Drythelm is attacked at one point by devils, but he is rescued by his guide. One of the more remarkable features of this vision is Drythelm's visit to the mouth of hell where he sees globes of fire, containing souls of the dead, rising and falling. Between heaven and hell there is a place where souls not worthy of being immediately admitted to heaven await a favorable judgment. This region is an early precursor of purgatory.

Drythelm returns to earth to live a good life and to show others how to do the same. He divides his wealth among his family and the poor and enters a monastery. His vision makes a point of the efficacy of the prayers, alms, fasting, and Masses of the living for the dead, since it is through these that those souls not quite worthy of heaven are eventually advanced to heaven.

The *Vision of the Monk of Melrose* by Helinand de Froidmont in *Chronicon* is based on *Drythelm's Vision*. A version can also be found as vision 20 in the *Liber visionum* of Otloh of Emmeran.

Sources
325   Ciccarese, see **13**, pp. 302–323.

Latin text based on Colgrave (**326**) with facing Italian translation. Includes brief introduction on the nature of this work with regard to the others in the collection. Provides some notes (332–36) to the text.

326   Colgrave, Bertram, and R. A. B. Mynors, ed. *Bede's Ecclesiastical History of the English People.* Oxford: Clarendon Press, 1969, 488–98.

Parallel Latin text and English translation with English notes. Select bibliography includes editions, critical works, translations of the *Historia,* and editions of sources used by Bede.

327   Gardiner, see **32**, pp. 57–63.

Includes an English translation of the vision with notes and bibliography.

328   Giles, J. A., ed. *The Miscellaneous Works of Venerable Bede.* 12 vols. London: Whittaker, 1843, 3: 200–13.

Latin critical edition with facing English translation.

329   PL 146:380 –83.

A Latin edition of Otloh of Emmeran's *Liber visionum.* Vision 20 of this book is the *VD* from Bede's *Historia.*

330   PL 95:247–52.

Text of *VD* in Latin edition of Bede's *Historia.*

331   Plummer, Charles, ed. *Venerabilis Baedae. Historiam Ecclesiasticam Gentis Anglorum.* Oxford: Clarendon, 1896, 1:303–10, 2:294–98.

Latin critical edition in volume 1; commentary in English in volume 2. Introduction, in English, discusses Bede's life and work and the mss of the *Historiam.*

332   Roger of Wendover. *Chronica, sive Flores historiarum.* Edited by Henry O. Coxe. 3 vols. London: English Historical Society, 1841; rpt. Vaduz: Kraus, 1964, 1:190–95.

Diplomatic edition of Latin text with annotations.

333   Roger of Wendover. *Flowers of History.* Edited by J. A. Giles. 2 vols. Bohn: London, 1849; rpt. New York: AMS, 1968, 1:120–22.

English translation based on Coxe edition (**332**); preface discusses Roger, the nature of his work, and his sources.

Studies

334   Wallace-Hadrill, J. M. *Bede's Ecclesiastical History of the English People: A Historical Commentary.* Oxford: Clarendon Press, New York: Oxford University Press, 1988, 185–86.

A commentary on the text of the *Historia,* which includes an extensive bibliography.

THE VISION OF AN ENGLISH NOVICE (VISIO CUIUSDAM NOUICII RAPTI IN PARTIBUS ANGLIA DE PURGATORIO)

Also called the *Vision of an English Man.* Written in Latin, not before the last decade of the twelfth century. From ms St. Gall, Stiftsbibliothek 142 (324–44), later incorporated in part into Vincent of Beauvais' *Speculum morale.*, where it is attributed to Peter of Cluny. A vision of purgatory where the visionary, led by St. Nicholas, sees, among other things, the punishments of a drunkard, of a knight who was too fond of hawking, of an insincere crusader, and of a knight who sold the presentment of a church in his patronage.

Sources
335   Vincent of Beauvais, see, **139**, vol. 3 (*Speculum morale*): 739.

Latin text in Book 2, Distinctio II, part I.

Studies
336   Constable, see, **379**, p. 95.

Brief mention.

THE VISION OF AN ENGLISH PRESBYTER (VISIO CUIUSDAM RELIGIOSI PRAESBITERI DE TERRA ANGLORUM)

Included by Prudentius of Troyes (835–61 CE) for the date 839 in the Annals of Saint-Bertin, *Annales Bertiniani,* (which is part of the *Annales regni Francorum*) named for one of the mss in which it is preserved, at the Abbey of Saint-Bertin. The *Vision of the English Presbyter,* in colloquial Latin and about 350 words long, takes place after Christmas, when an unnamed guide, who also answers his questions, leads him from his bed to a place where youths read from books where the sins of Christians are written in red. These youths intercede for the salvation of these Christians, and the priest is warned that if there is no repentance on earth, in three days all would be destroyed.

Sources
337   Grat, Felix, Jeanne Vielliard, and Suzanne Clémencet, ed. *Annales de Saint-Bertin.* Intro. and notes by Léon Levilain. Paris: Klincksieck, 1964, 29–30.

Critical edition of Latin text. Introduction in French covers the work, mss, other annals, sources for the *Annals de Saint-Bertin,* textual comparison of mss. and sources. Includes a bibliographic essay, which focuses mainly on early editions and translations.

338   MGH SRG 1:433–34.

Latin critical edition of the *Annales Bertiniani by* Prudentius of Troyes.

339   PL 115:1385.

> Edition of Latin text.

THE VISION OF EZRA (VISIO BEATI ESDRAE)

This Latin vision of heaven and hell, with the earliest manuscript dating from the tenth-eleventh century, is related to the apocalyptic *Fourth Book of Ezra* and therefore within this genre is closely related to the *Visio Pauli*. The *VE* is also related to two later works, the Greek *Apocalypsis Esdrae* and the Greek *Apocalypsis Sedrach*. Although the Latin *Visio* may be a translation from the Greek, there is some doubt on this point.

Ezra prayed to Christ for a vision of the judgment of sins and was led to the otherworld by seven angels. One angel acts as his guide and shows him those saved through works of charity. He also is shown the pains of hell, where sinners are punished in flames and by hanging, in pains that are suited to their sins. Ezra prays for the sinners throughout his journey through hell. Although hell is rather superficially described in this brief vision. A unique feature of this work is the discussion of his movements through the otherworld in terms of specifc numbers of steps through hell. Gabriel, Raphael, and Michael lead him to heaven. There he meets God and what follows includes a discussion of the fate of the human soul, a description of the physiogomy of the Anti-Christ, and a dispute between Ezra and the angel who was sent to take his soul.

The bibliography below concentrates on the medieval Latin *Visio Ezra* and does not attempt to organize the large body of material on the biblical or Greek sources.

Sources

340   Bogaert, Pierre-Maurice. "Un version longue inédite de la *Visio beati Esdrae.*" *Revue Benedictine* 94:1–2 (1984): 50–70.

Annotated Latin text of Barberini Lat. 2318 with lexicon. Introduction on text and ms tradition especially in the light of the version presented in the long edition and its relationship to other versions.

341   ———. "Anecdota apocrypha latina. Una 'Visio' ed una 'Revelatio' d'Esdra con un decreto di Clemente Romano." *Nota di letteratura biblica e cristiana antica.* Studi e testi 5. Rome: Vatican, 1901, 61–81.

Presents Latin texts with brief introduction

342   Mussafia, see **664**, appendix, 202–6.

Includes an edition of the Latin text.

343   Shutt, R. J. H. "Visio Beati Esdrae." In *Apocryphal Old Testament.* Ed. by H. S. Sparks. New York: Oxford University Press, 1984, 947–51.

English translation of Latin text with brief introduction.

344   Wahl, Otto, ed. *Apocalypsis Esdrae, Apocalypsis Sedrach, Visio Beati Esdrae.* Pseudepigrapha Veteris Testamenti Graece 4. Leiden: E. J. Brill, 1977.

Includes bibliography; introduction discusses mss, editorial method, other versions (Syrian, Arabic, Ethiopian, Armenian). Presents editions of Greek *Apocalypsis Esdrae* and *Apocalypsis Sedrach* and of Latin *Visio Beati Esdrae* and *Visio Esdrae* in facing columns. Review by Pierre-Maurice Bogaert, *Scriptorium* 33 (1979): 120–21.

Studies

345   Bratke, Prof. "Beatus v. Libana, Hieronymus und die Visio Hesdrae." *Zeitschrift für Kirchengeschichte* 23 (1902): 429–30.

      Brief review article.

346   Dinzelbacher, see **100**.

      Discusses the Vision of Alberic in the context of apocryphal literature and especially the Visio Esdrae, with a brief textual comparison.

347   Seymour, see **65**.

      Discusses a tradition in the literature of dying where the soul is unwilling or unable to leave the body through certain members (mouth, nose, etc.) either because they are sanctified (in the case of the righteous person) or are guarded by devils (in the case of sinners). Mentions two visions of the otherworld in this context, *Vision of St. Paul* and the *Vision of Ezra*.

348   Stone, M. E. "The Metamorphosis of Ezra: Jewish Apocalypse and Medieval Vision." *Journal of Theological Studies* n.s. 33 (1982): 1–18.

      Discusses the Fourth Book of Ezra and the relationship of various other Ezra materials to it and to each other, including: the Greek *Esdrae Apocalypse,* the Greek *Sedrach Apocalypse,* and, the *Visio Beati Esdrae.*

349   Wahl, Otto. "Vier Neue Textzeugen der 'Visio beati Esdrae.'" *Salesianum* 40:3 (1978): 583–90.

      Discusses four mss and the ms recensions.

THE VISION OF FURSEUS (VITA VIRTUTESQUE FURSEI ABBATIS LATINIACENSIS)

This vision apparently occurred in 633 CE, since it is included under that date in Bede's *Historia Ecclesiastica Gentis Anglorum* (Bk. 3, chap. 19), which was written in 731 in England in Latin. Bede's version is based on an Latin *vita* of unknown authorship. The vision also found independent of *HEGA* embedded in his Furseus's *vita* which consists mostly of his *visio*. It is about 100 words in length and recalls the *Book of Enoch* in its four-fold division of hell. Later versions of this vision are included in the *Legenda aurea* and in Vincent of Beauvais.

Like many visions this one has its origins in Ireland, which is where Furseus comes from. The vision, in this case a series of visions, actually occurs while he is in the province of the East Saxons. Furseus is a holy man who is occupied with preaching the Gospels. Of his three visions, the most significant is the third in which he sees combat among the evil spirits, is accused of evil by devils, is led up high by the three angels where he sees the four fires that will kindle and consume the world — falsehood, covetousness, discord, and iniquity. The three angels act as guides, but they are not very clearly drawn.

This is the earliest example of the punishment of a visionary. A devil throws the soul of a sinner at Furseus because he once received a garment from this sinner. Furseus' shoulder and jaw are burned. When Furseus returns to life he bears the mark of this burn.

Although after his vision he exhorts all to practice virtue, he tells his tale only to those most likely to profit from it. Physically affected by his vision, he wears only a thin garment and sweats even during East Anglian winters.

Sources

350   AS 2 January 16, 36–41.

        Edition of Latin text of *vita*.

351   Ciccarese, Maria Pia. "Le Visioni di S. Fursa." *Romano barbarica* 8. Rome: Herder, 1984–85, 231–303.

        Critical Latin edition of the *Vita sancti Fursei*, as a corrective to the Krusch edition (MGH Script. rerum Merov. 4:423–51) which omits the visions. Introduction includes *stemma codicum* and discussion of ms tradition and the more significant textual variants, as well as a discussion of the life of Furseus and the relationship between his vision and his life.

352   ———, see **13**, pp. 394–401.

        Latin text based on Ciccarese (see **351**) with facing Italian translation. Includes brief introduction on the nature of this work with regard to the others in the collection. Provides some notes to the text.

353   Colgrave, see **326**, pp. 268–77.

        Parallel Latin text and English translation with English notes. Select bibliography includes editions, critical works, translations of the *Historia*, and editions of sources used by Bede.

354   Gardiner, see **32**, pp. 51–55.

        Includes English translation of vision with notes and bibliography.

355   Giles, see **328**, 2:236–39.

         Latin critical edition with facing English translation.

356   PL 95:145–49.

         Text of *VF* in edition of Latin text. Bede's *Historia.*

357   Plummer, see **331**, 1:164–67, 2:169–74.

         Latin critical edition in volume 1; commentary in
         volume 2. Introduction, in English, discusses Bede's life
         and work and the mss of the *Historiam.*

Studies
358   Foster, see **29**, 22:456, 648.

         Description and bibliography of the Middle English
         Vision of Fursey (Furseus).

359   Wallace-Hadrill, J. M. *Bede's Ecclesiastical History of
         the English People: A Historical Commentary.*
         Oxford: Clarendon Press; New York: Oxford
         University Press, 1988, 185–86.

         A commentary on the text of the *Historia,* which
         includes an extensive bibliography.

THE VISION OF A GERMAN COUNT

A vision of hell recounted by Hildebrand (Gregory VII) before he became pope in 1073. The visionary is anonymous. In hell he sees a count who had died ten years previously He stands on a ladder with his ancestors below him and his descendants entering above him, and they descend rung by rung into the pit of hell. The sermon was recorded by Peter Damian.

Sources

360   Vossler, K. *La fonte della 'Divina Commedia' studiata nella sue genesi e interpretata.* Bari: P. unk., 1927, 1:186–87.

Not seen.

361   Ovidio, Francesco d'. *Studii sulla "Divina Commedia."* Caserta: Moderna, 1931, 297.

Not seen.

THE VISION OF GOTTSCHALK (VISIO GODESCHALCI)

Latin vision of heaven, purgatory, and hell written in 1189–90 by an anonymous redactor, which survives in an incomplete form of about 95,000 words. Gottschalk, a peasant from Holstein, lies as if dead from Christmas Eve 1188, until the fourth day of Christmas. During his trance he is guided through the otherworld by two angels. He is shown a tree of shoes, which are awarded to the merciful so that they might walk across the thorny moor unharmed. Initially Gottschalk is not given shoes, and after his return to life he bears the marks of his punishment. At one point, however, one of his guides takes mercy on him and returns for a pair of shoes.

There is a river of spikes which must be crossed either by swimming or by hanging onto a board floating by. On the other side of this broad river there are there paths: one to hell, one to purgatory, and the last to heaven. Gottschalk is led down all three. On the road to hell he sees people punished in their offending parts. The middle road of purgatory is broad and sweet, and it leads to the third heaven where Gottschalk sees a large shining church, and recognizes many known to him from life, bringing back from one of them a message for the son of one of the blessed. After he returns, Gottschalk tells his vision to a cleric who records it.

This vision has remarkable similarities with the *Vision of Olav Asteson (Draumkvaede)*, and has been linked to that vision as a possible source. Several features, like the tree of shoes, are quite unusual, as is the realism of characters and vignettes.

Sources
362   Assmann, Erwin. *Godeschalcus und Visio Godeschalci.* Quellen und Forschungen zur Geschichte Schleswig-

Holsteins 74. Neumünster: Karl Wachholtz Verlag, 1979.

Introduction includes a discussion of Gottschalk and his vision, the transmission of the story, the three mss, the printed editions, and the author of the two Latin versions edited here, one following the other, with facing translations into German. Includes a discussion of editorial method and linguistic notes on the language, style, and vocabulary.

363 Rockelein, see 62.

Combines psychological and ethnological approach in a study of Otloh of Emmeran with particular reference to the "collective" visions of *Gottschalk, Thurkill, Tundale,* and *Owayne (St. Patrick's Purgatory).*

364 Usener, R., ed. *Quellensammlung für Schleswig-holsteinisch-lauenburgische Geschichte* 4 (1875): 73–126.

Not seen.

365 Unsinger, R., ed. *"Visio Godeschalchi."* In *Scriptores minores rerum Slesvico-Holtsatensium.* Kiel: P. unk., 1875, 89–126.

Not seen.

Studies
366 Greven, Joseph. "Die Vision des Holsteiners Gottschalk." *Deutsches Dante-Jahrbuch* 7 (1923): 39–58.

Discusses the two versions of the *VG* in the light of the relationship of vision literature to the *Divine Comedy.*

367   Gurevich, A. "Oral and Written Culture of the Middle Ages: Two 'Peasant Visions' of the Late Twelfth-Early Thirteenth Centuries." Tr. by Ann Shukman. *New Literary History* 16 (1984): 51–66.

Discusses the problem of the interrelationship of oral and written traditions in the *Visio Thurkilli* and the *VG,* which are in constant and complex interaction.

368   Lammers, Walther. "Gottschalks wanderung im Jenseits. Zur Folksfrömmigkeit im 12. Jahrhundert nördlich der Elbe." Diss.: Goethe University, Frankfurt; Wesibaden: P. unk., 1962.

Not seen.

369   Liestøl, see **433,** pp. 91–96.

Synopsis of the *VG* and a discussion of it as a possible source for the *Vision of Olav Asteson* (*Draumkvaede*).

THE DIALOGUES OF ST. GREGORY THE GREAT
THE VISION OF PETER
THE VISION OF A SOLDIER
THE VISION OF STEPHEN

These short visions are from Bk. 4, ch. 37 of the *Dialogues* of Pope Gregory I (the Great, 540?–604), which were written in 593–94 in Latin.

These visions appear amid a discussion of the nature of heaven and hell, and each of them illustrates a different way in which one might be affected by a vision of the otherworld. The first visionary, Peter, dies and sees many torments. He is just about to be cast into them when an angel sends him back to earth. He converts and leads a good life.

The second visionary, Stephen, sees "many things" in the dungeon of hell, but the judge had wanted another Stephen, so this Stephen gets sent back to earth. His repentance is rather weak, as we learn from what the next visionary saw.

This was a soldier who left his body and saw in the otherworld the steward of the pope's family bound by a weight of iron because he was a sadist. He also saw the above-mentioned Stephen on a bridge being pulled up because of his charity and down because of his impurity. The soldier wakes without knowing what happens to Stephen.

None of these visionaries suffers during his vision, which is generally sent as a warning. Since these are not fully developed visions, but mere glimpses, we have neither a full range of sins covered nor a wide range of punishments; nor is the geography of the otherworld very well-defined. Only the soldier attempts some description of the topography of the otherworld. None of these visionaries is accompanied by a guide, although we do find the visionary meeting near-contemporaries in the otherworld. The visionaries are average people, neither saints with special

111

authority, nor the religious men who became very popular as visionaries in the later Middle Ages.

Gregory concludes that visions are sometimes for the benefit of those who see them and sometimes for the benefit of those who learn of them. Sometimes those who see these tortures amend their lives and avoid hell. Others, who do not, are tortured all the more.

Sources

370   De Vogüé, Adalbert, ed. *Gregoire le Grand: Dialogues.* Trans. by Paul Antin. 3 vols. Paris: Cerf, 1978–80, 3:116–125.

Annotated Latin critical edition with facing French translation. Vol. 1 includes an introduction and bibliography.

371   Gardiner, see **32**, pp. 47–50.

Includes English translation of visions with notes and bibliography.

372   Gardner, Edmund, ed. *The Dialogues of Saint Gregory.* London: Philip Lee Warner, 1911, 223–26.

English translation. General introduction on the *Dialogues,* their sources, influences, and transmission. Briefly mentions (p. xxv) the beginning of the western tradition of visions of heaven and hell in Gregory's *Dialogues.*

373   *The Dialogues of S. Gregorie.* Ilkley (England): Scolar Press, 1975.

Not seen.

374 Gregory the Great. *Dialogues.* Trans. by Odo John Zimmerman. New York: Fathers of the Church, 1959, 237–41.

 English translation, with a few annotations, based on Moricca's edition (**375**). Introduction provides a brief biography of Gregory and a brief introduction to the dialogues.

375 Moricca, Umberto, ed. *Gregorii Magni Dialogi.* Istituto storico italiano: Fonti per la storia d'Italia 57. Rome: Tip. del Senato, 1924.

 Critical edition of Latin text based primarily on Milan, Ambrosiana B. 159 sup. Introduction covers the date of composition; authenticity, scope and nature of the dialogues; the sources for the dialogues; the locations of the miracles; chronological determination of some of the miracles; the contents of the dialogues; the dialogues as a historical source; editions and manuscripts.

376 PL 77:381–88.

 Annotated edition of text in Latin and Greek in facing columns.

Studies

377 Gatch, Milton McC. "The Fourth Dialogue of Gregory the Great: Some Problems of Interpretation." In *Studia Patristica* 10, part 1. Ed. by F. L. Cross. Berlin: Akademie-Verlag, 1970, 77–83.

 Discusses the idea of purgatory in relation to Bk. 4 of Gregory's *Dialogues* where the idea of post-mortem purgation is clearly presented. Gatch believes this is not the early beginning of the formulation of the concept of a

Christian purgatory but a view of the Last Judgment temporally telescoped by Gregory's belief that he is living in the age of the apocalypse. Gatch sees the *Dialogues* as a popular work by Gregory and not really a serious theological treatise from which to derive doctrinal developments.

378   Petersen, Joan M. *The Dialogues of Gregory the Great in Their Late Antique Cultural Background.* Studies and Texts 69. Toronto: Pontifical Institute, 1984.

A reassessment of the *Dialogues* in relation to their sixth-century literary and theological background and to modern hagiographical research. Discusses particularly form and interpretation, the martyr stories, the miracle stories, relics and the spirituality of the desert. Extensive bibliography on primary sources and secondary works.

379   Silverstein, see **398**.

Discusses the bridge in *Leofric*, which resembles somewhat the bridge in a later (fourth century) Latin redaction of the *Visio Pauli*. However, he concludes, it is clearly dependent on the bridge in the *Dialogues* of Gregory the Great and therefore does not present a reason to suspect an earlier date of composition for this redaction of the *VP*.

THE VISION OF GUIBERT OF NOGENT'S MOTHER

Included in the *De vita sua* (Bk. 1, ch. 18) of Guibert (1053–1124), the abbot of Benedictine abbey of Nogent-sous-Coucy. Written in Latin c. 1116, in about 850, words. he tells of his mother's vision.

Guibert's mother, while taking a nap on a Sunday morning, experiences the separation of her soul from her body, although she maintains she had her senses. She travels through a long hallway, finding at the end a pit, where she is attacked by devils. She sees several people in her vision, including her husband, a friend of hers, and a knight named Renaud who died the very same day. All are condemned to suffer in the otherworld. But her vision of her husband leads her to spend the rest of her life in prayers and good deeds to relieve his suffering soul.

Sources

370   Benton, John F. *Self and Society in Medieval France.* New York: Harper & Row, 1970, 93–97.

English translation (based on the translaton of Bland, **371**) of the memoirs of Abbot Guibert of Nogent, with introduction.

371   Bland, C. C. Swinton. *The Autobiography of Guibert of Nogent.* Intro. by G. G. Coulton. London: Routledge, New York: Broadway Translations, 1925, 73–79.

Not seen. English translation of Latin text.

372   Bourgin, Georges, ed. *Guibert de Nogent: Histoire de sa Vie. Collection de textes pour servir à l'étude et à l'enseignement de l'histoire.* Paris: Picard, 1907.

Not seen. Modern edition of Latin text.

373   Le Goff, Jacques. *The Birth of Purgatory*. Translated by
        Arthur Goldhammer. Chicago: Chicago University
        Press, 1984 (originally published as *La naissance du
        purgatoire*. Paris: Gallimard, 1981), pp. 181–86.

        In the context of a study on the development of
        Purgatory in the twelfth century and the relationship of
        that development to the social history of the period., a
        brief discussion of the importance of the Guibert text with
        an English translation based on the translation in Benton
        (**370**).

374   PL 156:876–77.

        Edition of the Latin text of *Guibert abbatis De Vita
        sua libri tres*.

Studies
375   McLaughlin, Mary M. "Survivors and Surrogates:
        Children of Parents from the Ninth to the Twelfth
        Centuies." *The History of Childhood*. Ed. by Lloyd
        deMause. New York: Psychohistory Press, 1975,
        101–81.

        Discusses the childhood of Guibert and his
        relationship to his mother.

376   Paul, J. "Le démoniaque et l'imaginaire dans le De Vita
        sua de Guibert de Nogent." In *Le Diable au Moyen
        Age*. Senefiance 6. Aix-en-Provence: CUERMA,
        Paris: H. Champion, 1979, 371–99.

        Discusses the presence of the devil in Guibert's
        work, which should not be interpreted as an effort by the

clergy to edify the laity but as a reflection of a real belief in the devil.

THE VISION OF GUNTHELM

Also called the Vision of a Cistercian Novice, possibly by Peter the Venerable (d. 1156), but certainly by someone living in France. It was later included in an abbreviated version in Helinand's Chronicle (Bk. 48) where he dates it to 1161 and, based on Helinand's *Chronicle,* in Vincent of Beauvais' *Speculum Historiale* dated 1187 as "The Vision of a Cistercian Novice." The visionary is an English monk named William (Gunthelm, or Gunthelin, or Gundelin), and the vision may have taken place at Rievaulx (Yorkshire).

The visionary is taken up to heaven by St. Benedict where he sees a fair and shining city. There is a chapel full of people and the Virgin Mary, who bids St. Benedict to take Gunthelm back. He meets a monk from his own monastery, and afterwards the archangel Raphael leads Gunthelm to paradise—a place with a golden castle, a fair gate, fragrant herbs, glorious fruit, and jubilant birds. He sees Adam, the father of all mankind. Then Raphael leads him to darks places full of the shadows of death, where he sees gloomy towers, which are the chimneys of hell. He sees people, including clerics of various types, seated in chairs tortured, and Raphael, acting as guide, explains their tortures. Finally, in the abyss of hell, Gunthelm sees Judas.

One unusual aspect of this vision is that it is supposed to be strictly personal and the visionary is not meant to reveal what he has seen.

This vision, of approximately 3000 words, has been discussed by Constable (**378**) in the context of the controversy between the Cistercians and Cluniacs.

Sources

377   Constable, Giles, ed. "The Vision of a Cistercian Novice." *Studia Anselmiana* 40 (1956): 95–98.

Not seen. Edition of Latin text.

378   ——, ed. "The Vision of a Cistercian Novice." In
        Petrus Venerabilis, 1156–1956. Rome: Herder,
        1956, 95–96.

        Diplomatic edition of Latin text from Cambridge,
        Sidney Sussex College 95. Introduction discusses the
        manuscript and the role of this vision in the controversy
        between the Cluniacs and the Cistercians and in the
        controversy between public and private confession.

379   ——, ed. "The Vision of Gunthelm and Other Visions
        Attributed to Peter the Venerable." *Revue Bénédictine*
        66 (1956): 92–114.

        Provides critical edition of *VG* and two visions of a
        monk of Savigny based on Brussels, B.R. II. 942 with
        variants from Copenhagen, Kongelige Bib. Gl. kgl. S.
        136; Paris B.N. Lat. 14463; St. Omer, Bibl. Mun. 328;
        and Brussels, B.R. 7797–806. Thorough introduction on
        the attribution of this work to Peter the Venerable (to
        whom several visions were attributed), its subsequent
        adaptation by Helinand and Vincent of Beauvais, its use
        in Mary legends, and its influence, especially on the
        Vision of Thurkill and the Vision of Olav Asteson. Rpt.
        with addenda in Giles Constable, *Cluniac Studies*
        (London: P. unk., 1980).

380   PL 212:1060–63.

        Edition of Latin text of Helinand's *Chronicle* without
        annotation.

381   Vincent of Beauvais,   see **139**, Vol. 4, *Speculum
        historiale,* 1187.

Bk. 29, ch. 6. Abbreviated version of the Latin *visio* called *De novicio Cisterciensi tenate à sathana.*

Studies

382   Liestøl, see **433**, pp. 87–91.

Synopsis of the *VG* and a discussion of it as a possible source for the *Vision of Olav Asteson* (*Draumkvaede*).

THE VISION OF HERIGER

Tenth- or eleventh-century Latin poetic satire in decasyllabic versi, 150 words, of otherworld visions recounted by a prophet who is called throughout a liar, to Heriger, archbishop of Mainz (912–26). He travels to hell, which he describes as surrounded by a wood, and to heaven where he describes the table where the abstemious John the Baptist serves the wine. It is the first example of satire in the afterlife tradition. Du Méril (**385**) suggests that its aim was to remove pagan elements from Christian belief.

Sources

383   Allen, Philip S., and Howard M. Jones, eds. *The Romanesque Lyric*. Chapel Hill, N.C.: University of North Carolina Press, 1928, 278–79.

English verse translation; unannotated. Describes VH as the "earliest known example of that happy-go-lucky attitude toward the saints and their celestial abode so popular in later centuries."

384   Breul, Karl. *The Cambridge Songs*. Cambridge: Cambridge University Press, 1915, 59–60.

Unannotated Latin text.

385   Du Méril, see **106**, pp. 298–302.

Annotated Latin edition.

386   Gaselee, Stephen, ed. *The Oxford Book of Medieval Latin Verse*. Oxford: Clarendon, 1928, 66–68.

Latin text.

387   Raby, F. J. E., ed. *The Oxford Book of Medieval Latin Verse.* Oxford: Clarendon, 1959, 170–71.

Latin text.

388   Waddell, Helen. *Medieval Latin Lyrics.* New York: Henry Holt & Co., 1933, 148–55.

English verse translation with facing Latin from the ms of St. Augustine of Canterbury.

THE VISION OF JOHN, MONK OF ST. LAWRENCE OF LIEGE

Latin vision of heaven and hell, dated 1148–58. After an illness John visits the otherworld guided by his patron saint, Lawrence. He begins his visit at purgatory where he sees a group of monks sitting together suffering through privation of angels, light, and hope. These souls eventually progress through purgatory aided by the intercession of their patron saints and the faithful. John visits heaven where he encounters a great temple from which issue songs and music. Finally the temple disappears and John is led through the infernal regions by St. Maurice, eventually returning to his body.

Sources
389   PL 180:177–86.

Edition of Latin text of 1147.

THE VISION OF LAISRÉN

Laisrén was probably abbot of Lethglenn (Leighlin), Carlow, d. 638. This vision is in Old Irish and a fragment of his visit to hell is all that remains. The work dates from early tenth, or perhaps latter half of ninth century.

At the end of three days' fast Laisrén experiences his soul leaving his body and being taken up by two angels. He is brought before a host of angels who are confronted by a host of devils — black ones with spears, dark brown ones with darts, and shaggy hairy ones with javelins. The devils argue that they should have him, but the angels tell them that he is not here to stay, but only so he can warn his friends about the afterlife. An angel, who hold a dialogue with Laisrén, takes him to hell where he sees a pit between two mountains, which they enter and from there proceed to the Mouth of Hell, where he sees the souls of those who will be damned if they don't repent. He is led on to hell itself, which is a sea of fire with an unspeakable storm and waves. Here souls are pierced through their sinning bodily parts with nails. But suddenly the vision breaks off.

Sources

390   Meyer, Kuno, ed. and trans. "The Vision of Laisrén." *Otia Merseiana* 1 (1899): 113–19.

        Presents an edition of the Irish text and a translation into English, with notes, from Oxford, Bodleian Rawlinson B. 512, a fifteenth-century manuscript.

Studies

391   Grosjean, Paul. "Notes d'hagiographique celtique: Un fragment des Costumes de Tallaght et la Vision de

Laisrén." *Analecta Bollandiana* 81.1–2 (1963): 251–72.

Discusses text found in Stowe C.1.2 of the Royal Irish Academy (Dublin), which contains a fragment of *VL* and discusses primarily the dating of the work based on this Irish text, referring to Meyer's work (**390**).

THE VISION OF LAZARUS (VISIO LAZARI)

Fifteenth-century vision of hell in which Lazarus recounts what he had seen in the otherworld before Christ raised him from the dead.

This vision does not provide a specific sense of place, but rather describes seven scenarios for punishing the seven deadly sins: the proud turned on wheels, the envious in a frozen lake, the ireful butchered in a shadowy cave, the slothful tormented by serpents, the covetous boiled in cauldrons of molten metal, the gluttons fed with disgusting beasts, and finally the lecherous tormented in wells of fire and sulphur. Although each description is brief it is vivid, and each description is followed by a sermon-like meditation on the particular sin.

This work obviously differs from the other texts in the circumstances, the historical character of the visionary, and the nature of the "authenticity" of the vision. There is nothing personal in this vision that makes Lazarus more real, and since he has no guide and meets no one known to him, there is no discussion to enliven the vision.

Sources

392   Voigt, Max. *Beiträge zur Geschichte der Visionen-literatur im Mittelalter.* Leipzig: Mayer & Müller, 1924; rpt. New York: Johnson Reprint, 1967, 1–118.

       Edition of the German text with notes. Introduction includes material on the Lazarus legend, the antecedents for this vision, the mss, and the language of the mss.

393   Heseltine, G. C., ed. *The Kalendar and Compost of Shepherds.* London: P. Davies, 1930, 59–67.

This edition of the Shepherd's Calendar is "From the original edition published by Guy Marchant in Paris in the year 1493, and translated into English c. 1518; newly edited, for the year 1931." This calendar incorporates a version of the *VL.*

THE VISION OF LEOFRIC

This vision of heaven of Leofric, Earl of Mercia (d. 1057), dates from late eleventh century, written in Old English prose.

In a half-sleeping state Leofric crosses a bridge and meets an unnamed guide who leads him through a fair field full of crowds in snow-white garments. He sees St. Paul who is finishing Mass, and then he meets six venerable men, one of whom asks what this foul man is doing among them. Another of the six answers that Leofric has been baptized again by penitence, and he will join them in heaven on the third "gelyrd-tid." This work continues to tell of three miraculous incidents during the life of Leofric and his own prediction of his death a fortnight before it.

Sources
394   Napier, A.S., ed. "An Old English 'Vision of Leofric,' Earl of Mercia." *Transactions of the Philological Society* 1907–1910:180–88.

Diplomatic edition of Old English text based in Cambridge, Corpus Christi College 367, with introduction on ms and dialect.

Studies
395   Gerould, G.H. *Saints Legends.* Boston and New York: Houghton Mifflin, 1916; rpt. Folcroft, Pa.: Folcroft Press, 1969, 126.

In a brief mention of the *VL*, the author described it as "an account of more than one supernatural manifestation....Most interesting is his vision of the bridge of souls, a borrowing from the *Vision of St. Paul*, which was to be popularized in Middle English times." (See **398**.)

396   Foster, see **29**, 2:456, 648.

Description and bibliography on the *Vision of Leofric.*

397   Pulsiano, Phillip. "Hortatory Purpose in the OE *Visio Leofrici.*" *Medium Aevum* 44 (1985): 109–16.

Author argues that although this work might appear to be a pastiche of four loosely connected episodes, "the author of the *Visio* subtly balances and contrasts the sinful life with the eternal life in God's company."

398   Silverstein, Theodore. "The 'Vision of Leofric' and Gregory's Dialogues." *Review of English Studies* 9 (April 1933): 186–88.

Discusses the bridge in *Leofric*, which resembles somewhat the bridge in a later Latin redaction of the *Visio Pauli*. However, he concludes, it is clearly dependent on the bridge in the *Dialogues* of Gregory the Great and therefore does not present a reason to suspect an earlier date of composition for this redaction of the *VP*.

THE VISION OF MARGUERITE D'OINGT

This lovely vision of heaven appears in Marguerite d'Oingt's *Speculum*, her spiritual autobiography, which she wrote in Latin before her death in 1310. Although it is autobiographical, Marguerite often describes her experiences in the third person.

This brief vision, her second, is actually a stunning description that avoids concrete physical description and concentrates on describing the emotional state of one experiencing heaven, of wholeness, well-being, and love. Both sweetness and love are used to convey the sense of heaven. One of the most remarkable images describes the saints' relationship to their creator in heaven as "fish within the sea."

Sources

399   Duraffour, Antonin, Pierre Gardette, and Paulette Durdilly, eds. *Marguerite d'Oingt: Édition critique de ses oeuvres.* Paris: Les Belles Lettres, 1965.

Not seen. According to Petroff (**60**) "The only modern edition of her works . . . based in part on earlier transcriptions collated with other manuscripts."

400   Petroff, see **60**, pp. 292.

Translation of selection of the *Speculum*, which includes this vision, plus an introduction on the visionary (pp. 277–80).

THE VISION OF MAXIMUS (DE MAXIMO MONACHO QUI VALERIO VISIONEM PROPRIAM RETULIT DE PARADISI AMOENITATE, ET DE LAMENTIS BARATRI)

A Latin vision of heaven and hell, about 800 words long, written by Saint Valerius del Bierzo in a letter to a certain Donadus in 656, and included in Bk. 17–19 of his *Opere*. (See *Vision of Baldarius*.)

Valerio meets Maximus when, as a young man, Valerio visits a church. Maximus is part of the large congregation of monks. He explains to Valerio that an angel of light took him up to heaven and showed him its great beauty with flowers and trees and a delicious water. The angel asks him if there is similar water on earth and whether he finds this place pleasing.

Maximus answers both questions with great enthusiasm, telling the angel how he would like to remain there. But the angel then takes him to the horrid and terrible abyss of hell. He explains how he can see very little but can hear the great anguish. Afraid he will fall into the pit of hell, he asks the angel's help, and the angel asks him whether he would prefer the beauty of heaven or hell. He predictably answers that he prefers heaven, and the angel promises to bring him back to heaven if he returns to the world and leads a good life. The angel points him in a homeward direction, although he must pass three men on top of a mountain, one who writes, one who dictates, and one who carries a cudgel. They indicate his way, and he arrives at his monastery just in time to interrupt his funeral. He then leads a good life and again departs from his body.

Sources
401   Ciccarese, see **13**, pp. 280–87.

Latin text based on Pousa (**403**) with facing Italian translation. Includes brief introduction (pp. 276–79) on the nature of this work with regard to the others in the collection. Provides some notes (298–301) to the text.

402   PL 87:431–33.

Reprint of the diplomatic edition of the Latin text edited by Henrique Flórez et al., in *Espana sagrada,* 51 vols. (Madrid: Gabriel Ramirez, 1762), 16:379–82.

403   Pousa, see **126** , pp. 110–14.

Not seen. Critical edition.

Studies
404   Aherne, see **127**, pp. 57–61.

Brief discussion of the three visions (Baldarius, Bonellus, and Maximus) with comparison to Valerio's autobiographical writings and to each other. Each of the visions is apparently related to Valerio by the visionary himself. Claims that "the accounts of the three visions are among the most interesting of Valerio's writings." Includes a general, select bibliography on Valerio.

VISION OF MERLINO (FIS MERLINO)

Irish vision of a wicked man of Bohemia, Merlino Malignois who listens to a sermon that influences his mind. However, he is on his way to a tryst with a comrade when they meet a parade of nobles which they join. They proceed with them to the castle of an earl. When they enter this castle, where they had expected to find delight, they find hell – and Merlino's comrade reveals himself to be the Spirit of Knowledge. This vision, primarily of hell, describes the seven deadly sins as punished in the offending bodily parts. Various animals, such as snakes and adders are part of the tortures, which are quite marvelously described. For instance, the Lake of Pains is said to be horrible because "one single drop of the water of the lake would destroy all the creatures on the surface of the earth by the bitterness of its chill." There is ongoing dialogue between Merlino and the spirit on the nature of hell, its punishments, Lucifer, Beelzebub, repentance and mercy. There are very brief glimpses of purgatory and heaven, followed by Merlino's return to this world and his repentance, upon which he is shown the mercy of God.

Sources
405   Macalister, R.A. Stewart, ed. and trans. "The Vision of Merlino." *Zeitschrift für Celtische Philologie* 4 (1902–3): 394–455.

Provides a brief introduction which claims no knowledge of the origin of the work, mentions possible connection with Italian sources (with Virgil), and lists fourteen mss with brief descriptions. Presents a critical edition of the Irish text with a facing English translation.

406   ———. *Fis Merlino: The Vision of Merlino: An Irish Allegory*. Dublin: M.H. Gill, 1906.

This is a revision of the translation published in **405**. Presents the Irish text then the English translation, without introduction, followed by an Irish vocabulary.

THE VISION OF THE MONK OF BERNICIA

This vision, of about 400 words, is included in Bk. 5, ch. 14 of Bede's *Historia*. It follows another vision in ch. 13 of a man of Mercia (Vision of a Thane, 704–9 CE), which is not a vision of the otherworld, but more a visitation of devils and angels to the bedside of a suffering sinner.

The *Vision of the Monk of Bernicia* (between Tyne and Forth, later part of the kingdom of Northumbria), a vision of hell, is rarely discussed among visions of the otherworld. It is, however, a brief vision by a sinner, who sees the places reserved for his punishment after death. As a monk he led a loose and drunken life and did not participate in church services, but, as the text explains, he was kept on at the monastery because he was needed as a skilled smith.

In most of the other visions, with the exception of the "Vision of Stephen" from the *Dialogues* of Gregory the Great, repentence always follows the vision. This sinner, however, does not repent with the knowledge obtained from his vision. He immediately despairs and dies. Bede comments that although this monk's soul was not saved the story of his vision was instrumental in bringing to repentance many who heard his story, and so Bede has included this vision in his *Historia* in the hope of extending the beneficial effects of this story of despair even further.

Sources
407   Ciccarese, see **13**, pp. 328–31.

> Latin text based on Colgrave (**326**) with facing Italian translation. Includes brief introduction on the nature of this work with regard to the others in the collection. Provides some notes (p. 336) to the text.

408   Colgrave, see **326**, pp. 502–5

Parallel Latin text and English translation with English notes. Select bibliography includes editions, critical works, translations of the *Historia* and editions of sources used by Bede.

409   Giles, see **328**, pp. 3:218–23.

Latin critical edition with facing English translation.

410   PL 95:254–55.

Latin edition of Bede's *Historia.*

411   Plummer, see **331**, 1:313–15, 2:299–301.

Latin critical edition in volume 1; commentary in volume 2. Introduction, in English, discusses Bede's life and work and the mss. of the *Historia*.

Studies
412   Wallace-Hadrill, see **334**, 1p. 87.

A commentary on the text of the *Historia,* which includes an extensive bibliography.

THE VISION OF THE MONK OF EYNSHAM (VISIO MONACHI DE EYNSHAM)

A lengthy Latin vision of purgatory dated 1196. It was written, in about 22,000 words, in 1197 by order of the bishop of Lincoln. The redactor was Adam, subprior of the monastery, who was the brother of Edmund, the monk of Eynsham. The monk is never mentioned by name, but he is a very sick monk, who believes he is about to die. The vision is set in England at Eynsham near Oxford, according to Thurston, basing his evidence on Coggeshall and some of the mss of the Latin original. Here there was a rich Benedictine abbey dating from the eighth century.

The monk asks to be shown the afterlife beforehand. On the night before Good Friday his fellow monks find him and think he is dead. He begins to revive at midnight before Easter, and afterward he is persuaded to tell of his vision.

The monk is guided by St. Nicholas, who has little to say. The vision strongly promotes the idea of praying or offering Masses for the dead to help them through their own punishments.

The places of punishment include two plains and a hot and cold mountain above a stinking body of water. The sins and punishments are not matched for the reader although sinners are punished according to their sins. The work does mention that those punished most severely are those most honored in life. Particularly singled out are judges and prelates, but the worst punishments are reserved for a certain sexual sin. The visionary says that this sin is so awful he will not even mention it, and he claims that he never knew of its existence before this vision.

The visionary also singles out for attention a particular lawyer who robbed his clients, neglected to repent before dying, and now despairs of the mercy of God. The monk meets some here whom he knows, including a goldsmith, who has been granted assistance by St. Nicholas, although those he knew on earth denied that he would obtain heaven. The monk is asked to pray for him after he returns.

The monk next sees the three places of glory, including the Heavenly Jerusalem, and a vision of Christ on the cross, before returning to life.

The visionary is not punished during his vision, but he is asked to tell his vision when he returns and to request the prayers of the living for the dead. The idea of working one's way through punishment toward reward is very prominent here, and there is no sense that any of the souls the monk meets are eternally damned.

This vision bears signs of influnce by the *Vision of Drythelm*. There are several extant mss of this version; and later accounts are included in the works of Roger of Wendover, Matthew Paris, and Ralph Coggeshall. It is cited as an authority in the *Vision of Thurkill.*

Sources

413   AB 22 (1903): 225–319.

Critical edition of Latin "Visio monachi de Eynsham" (pp. 236–319), ed. by Herbert Thurston. Introduction discusses the tradition of vision literature, the connection between this work and Hugh of Lincoln, and eight mss of the text.

414   Arber, Edward, ed. *The Revelation to the Monk of Evesham*. English Reprints 18. London: English Reprints, 1869; Westminster: A. Constable, 1895, 1901.

This edition in English is based on the one printed by William de Machlinia, c.1482. The editors do not know of mss and assume the work was originally written in English.

415   Gardiner, **32**, 197–218.

Includes English translation of vision with notes and bibliography.

416   Huber, Michael, ed. "Visio Monachi de Eynsham." *Romanische Forschungen* 16 (1904): 641–733.

Critical Latin edition based on Chartres Cod. Lat. 131 (84). Introduction mentions seven mss consulted to prepare this edition.

417   Paget, Valerian, trans. *The Revelation to the Monk of Evesham.* New York: McBride, 1909.

English translation with a general introduction on the historical and literary importance of the vision.

418   *Revelation of the Monk of Evesham: A Remarkable Psychological Production of the Middle Ages Now for the First Time Sufficiently Rendered into Present Day English.* Pleaknowe, Scotland: Thomson & Co., 1904.

Not seen.

419   Roger of Wendover, see **332**, 3:97–117.

Diplomatic edition of the Latin text with annotations.

420   Roger of Wendover, see **333**, 2: 148–64.

English translation based on Coxe edition (**332**). Preface discusses Roger, the nature of his work, and his sources.

421   Salter, H.E., ed. *Visio monachi de Eynsham. Eynsham Cartulary.* 2 vols. Oxford Historical Society

Publications 49, 51. Oxford: Oxford Historical Society, 1908, 2: 257–371.

Critical edition of the Latin text based on Digby Ms. 34. Introduction includes discussion of mss and a discussion of evidence for associating this work with Oxford, examining carefully first the identification of the visionary with St. Edmund, and eventually rejecting this identification and linking the vision to an unidentified monk who was a native of Oxford.

422   Ward, see **306**, 2(1893): 493–506.

Descriptions of Latin mss: Cotton Cleopatra C. xi, Cotton Caligula A. viii, Harley 3776.

Studies

423   Cosmo, Umberto. "Una nuova fonte dantesca?" *Studi medievali* 1 (1904–5): 77–93.

Speculation on the Visio monachi de Eynsham as a possible source for Dante through Matthew Paris. He acknowledges that there is no evidence, but asserts that it is not impossible that Dante might have come across this work as he almost surely did come across the *Vision of Furseus* and the *Vision of Drythelm.*

424   Davies, Constance. "The Revelation to the Monk of Evesham." *Review of English Studies* 11 (1935): 182–83.

Brief note maintaining the validity of the designation of "Evesham," about ten miles southwest of Stratford-on-Avon in Worcestershire.

425   Foster, see **29**, 2:457, 649.

Description and bibliography on the *Vision of the Monk of Eynsham.*

426   Thurston, Herbert. "The Vision of the Monk of Eynsham." *The Month* 91 (1898): 49–63.

Attempts to establish legitimacy for this vision based on the premise that the monk in question "was intimately associated with...St. Hugh of Avalon, bishop of Lincoln, and that the revelation was both approved by him, and even published at his express desire"; and that the vision was actually written down by Adam, Hugh's biographer. This theory is based on the prologue of Coggeshall to the *Vision of Thurkill.* Lists five mss of *VME* (554–55 notes).

THE VISION OF THE MONK OF MELROSE

This Latin vision is included in Helinand's *Chronicle* and dated 1160; it is based upon the *Vision of Drythelm,* with which it has great similarities.

The man is guided by a bright angel first to purgatory, then to the pit of hell, and finally to the forecourt of heaven and heaven itself. The visionary sees globes of fire ascending and descending, a detail found, otherwise exclusively, in Drythelm's vision. During the visit to the pit of hell, he is surrounded and taunted by devils but finally rescued by his guide.

The vision makes a point of the value of prayers, almsgiving, and Mass for salvation and the benefit of these when performed for the souls of the dead.

The visionary is returned unwillingly to life and enters the monastery of Melrose, where, like Drythelm, he is known to bathe in icy rivers in mid-winter, claiming that he has seen harsher pains.

Sources
426   PL 212:1059–60.

> Edition of Latin text from Helinand's *Chronicle* without annotation.

THE VISION OF THE MONK OF WENLOCK

This vision of the otherworld appears in a letter (716 CE) from St. Boniface (Winfrid) to Abbess Eadberga, abbess of Thanet, concerning a monk of the Abbey of Wenlock in Shropshire. Boniface heard this story and then spoke with the visionary himself before writing his letter, which records the vision in about 2500 words.

It begins when the monk is on the point of violent illness. As his spirit is freed from his body, he is guided upward by angels. He describes a marvelous vision of flames, by which he is injured, but healed by an angel. He sees the souls of the newly dead gathered together where angels and devils violently dispute over them. His own sins appear personified before him to attack him, but he is defended by his virtues personified.

This is essentially a vision of hell of purgation wherein devils and angels contend over the souls of the dead. The landscape is full of pits vomiting flames. Beneath this is a lower hell from which is heard an incredible weeping. The monk describes a bridge over a pitch-black, boiling river. Souls crossing over to paradise may fall from the bridge into the river where they are cleansed before reaching the far shore. He witnesses an attack by devils when they try to kidnap one of the blessed souls, but this soul is saved by angels, and the devils scatter, only to reform and try again to take another soul.

He also sees several of his contemporaries and is told to warn one of them to repent. Some of the things he sees are prophetic and serve as guarantees of the veracity of the vision.

The monk is sent back to his body and commanded to reveal what he had seen to those willing to believe him, but to avoid those who might scoff at him.

This vision may have been influenced by the Vision of Paul in its use of the immersion motif, and by Gregory the Great in the

143

bridge motif. It makes direct reference to the *Vision of Bernoldus* and is included in Otloh of Emmeran's *Liber visionum.*

Sources

427   Ciccarese, see **13**, pp. 337–65.

Latin text with facing Italian translation. Includes brief introduction on the nature of this work with regard to the others in the collection. Provides some notes to the text.

428   Emerton, Ephraim. *The Letters of St. Boniface.* Records of Civilization: Sources & Studies 31. New York: Columbia University Press, 1940, 25–31.

Presents an English translation based on the Kylie **(429)** translation. The introduction lists three of six mss, early editions, translations; gives a biographical account of Boniface and his period, and a general description of his correspondence.

429   Kylie, Edward. *The English Correspondence of St. Boniface.* King's Classics. London: Chatto & Windus, 1911, 78–89.

English translation of letters.

430   MGH Epistolae 3 (Merowingici et Karolini aevi 1) 252:57.

Edition of Latin text by E. Dümmler.

431   MGH Epistolae selectae 1(1916): 7–15.

Edition of Latin text by M. Tangl.

432   Rau, Reinhold, ed. *Briefe des Bonifatius; Willibalds Leben des Bonifatius.* Darmstadt: Wissenschaftliche Buchgesellschaft, 1968, 30–43.

Annotated edition of Latin text with facing German translation.

THE VISION OF OLAV ASTESON

Early thirteenth century Norwegian ballad. This dream of the otherworld lasts from Christmas Eve to the Epiphany. The dreamer, Olav Asteson, "a lad so brave and strong," visits the realm of the dead and views a preliminary judgment of sins by St. Michael. He sees the retribution for evil deeds and the reward for good deeds in a landscape that includes the Gjallar Bridge an important feature of this otherworld, is protected by a dog, a serpent, and a bull. He has no guide, but he does meet his "god mother," the only person he recognized there, and she does direct his wanderings in the otherworld. This "godmother" has been associated with the Mother of God.

This bibliography has made no attempt to cover the broad range of material in Norwegian on this work.

Sources
433   Liestøl, Knut, ed. *Draumkvaede: A Norwegian Visionary Poem from the Middle Ages.* Studia Norvegica 1 (1946) 3. Oslo: Aschenhoug (Nygaard), 1946.

Presents the two most important versions in Old Norse (pp. 134–41), and an English verse translation (pp. 7–16). Liestøl's study includes a thoroughgoing analysis of the vision motifs in the poem and the probable sources – Tundale, Gunthelm and Thurkill. He also discusses the name of the poem and the visionary, the different versions, parallels with and influence on other popular ballads, Norse matter, Anglo-Irish visionary literature, relations between England and Norway, and the author of the work.

146

Studies

434   Constable, see **379**, pp. 99–100.

Discusses the influence of the *Vision of Gunthelm* on the *Vision of Olav Asteson.*

435   Dinzelbacher, Peter. "Zur Entstehung vom Draum-kvaede." *Skandinavistik* 10 (1980): 89–96.

Traces the origins of this work in the tradition of eschatological and visionary literature.

THE VISION OF ORM

Orm, a youth, who died in 1126 has a vision in November 1125 of four places: heaven, paradise, outside the wall of paradise and hell. Written in Latin by Sigar of Newbald (Yorkshire) c. 1126., this is a simple vision, of about 1000 words, that "represents the beliefs of the parochial clergy and simple laity" in the twelfth century in northeast England.

This vision is of particular interest because of the extreme youth of the visionary (13 years old) and the close relationship of this vision to the *Vision of Drythelm.*

Orm becomes ill and is in a state of apparent death for thirteen days. He actually has three different visions. When he recovers, he describes the wall of paradise, over which he could look; the Mouth of Hell, where lost souls are tormented with heat and cold; and purgatory, where punishment is the knowledge of loss and deprivation.

In the first vision he sees Christ crucified, Mary, the apostles, and several people known to him; in the second vision he sees Christ and the Apostles, whose swords are two-thirds drawn, apocalyptically indicating that two-thirds of the world's history is over. Orm returns from his third vision via Rome and Jerusalem.

Sources
436   AB 75 (1957): 72–82.

An edition by Hugh Farmer of the unique Latin manuscript (Oxford, Bodleian Fairfax 17) with a brief introduction outlining the simple plot and introducing Orm and the author of his story. Comparisons are made to *Drythelm's Vision* in Bede's *Historia.*

THE VISION BOOK OF OTLOH OF EMMERAN
THE VISION OF A SERVANT
THE VISION OF THE MONK ISAAC
THE VISION OF A BEGGAR
THE VISION OF THE EMPRESS THEOPHANU

Seven visions of the otherworld are included among the twenty-three in the Latin *Liber visionem tum suarum, tum aliorum* of Otloh, a Benedictine monk of Ratisbon (Regensburg) in the eleventh century. Two of these are closely related to the *Vision of Drythelm* and the *Vision of the Monk of Wenlock*.

The sixth vision in this book is by a woman, a servant, who returns with news about the tribune Aldericus's parents.

The *Vision of a Beggar*, the eleventh vision in the collection, describes the experiences of a local beggar (about 600 words in length) who sees the recently dead in a metal house, an empty well surrounded by many unused paths, and a delapidated monastery before he is shown a dying tree, which represents the bishop.

The fourteenth vision is the *Vision of the Monk Isaac*, a monk of Bohemia, who meets the hermit Gunther in a beautiful place and also sees the mountain of hell and the place of judgement, whose seats of fire remind the reader of the theater in the *Vision of Thurkill*.

The *Vision of Empress Theophanu*, the seventeenth vision, concerns the fate of the empress in hell.

Sources
437   PL 146:341–88.

Edition of Latin text: Servant, 359–60; Monk Isaac, 368–70; Beggar, 368–70; Theophanu, 372–73.

149

Studies

438   Schauwecker, Helga. "Otloh von St. Emmeram. Ein Beitrag zur Bildungs and Frömmigkeit des 11 Jahrhunderts." Ph.D. Diss.: University of Wurzburg, 1962; rpt. *Studien und Mitteilungen zur Geschichte aus des Benediktiner-ordens* 7 (1963): 3–20.

Examines Otloh's work, life, and thought.

439   Philipp-Schawecker, Helga. "Othlo und die S. Emmeramer Fälschungen des 11 Jahrhunderts." *Historische Vereins für Oberpfalz und Regensburg, Verhandlungen* 106 (1966): 103–20.

Discusses the connection between Otloh, St. Emmeran, and Dionysian rites.

440   Rockelein, see **62**.

Combines psychological and ethnological approaches in a study of Otloh of Emmeran with particular reference to the "collective" visions of Gottschalk, Thurkill, Tundale, and Owein (*St. Patrick's Purgatory*).

441   Schröbler, Ingeborg. "Otloh von S. Emmeram und Hieronymus." *Beitrage zur Geschichte des Deutschen Sprache und Literatur* (Tubingen) 79 (1957): 335–62.

Not seen.

ST. PATRICK'S PURGATORY
THE VISION OF KNIGHT OWEIN (TRACTATUS DE PURGATORIO SANCTI PATRICII)
THE VISION OF WILLIAM STAUNTON
THE VISION OF LOUIS OF FRANCE (VISIO LUDOVICI DE FRANCIA)
THE VISION OF RAYMOND DE PEREHLOS
THE VISION OF LAURENCE RATHOLD
THE VISION OF GEORGE, KNIGHT OF HUNGARY, OR GEORGE GRISSOPHAN
THE VISION OF LAURENT DE PASZTHO

Patrick was a fifth-century saint, who lived in Ireland. Among the legends surrounding his life is the story of his vision of purgatory. This legend gave rise to the identification of the spot where the entrance to purgatory might be found, located on Station Island in the lake, Lough Derg, a popular pilgrimage site in northeast Limerick. Around this site many legends arose. The first and foremost is the story of the Knight Owein, told by H. of Sawtry (Saltry) in the *Tractatus de Purgatorio sancti Patricii* (c. 1179–81) in Latin. A French text was soon derived from the numerous Latin manuscripts, which are numerous. Of the French translations there are at least seven in verse – one by Marie de France – and at least as many prose versions. There are also translations into Provencal, English (including "Owayne Miles"), and Italian. Criticism focuses on the history of Lough Derg, the site of the Purgatory. Accounts of, or references to, this work occur in the works of Matthew Paris, Roger of Wendover, Jacobus de Voragine, Caesarius of Heisterbach, Jacopo of Vitriaco, Vincent of Beauvais, Etienne de Bourbon, and Peter the Venerable.

There are many different accounts of visits to St. Patrick's Purgatory, dating from when it was founded in c. 445 until 1497, when it was temporarily closed by Pope Alexander VI. Many who entered the little cave at Lough Derg and spent one evening or three there, told of visiting the Purgatory. But some of the works describing a visit to this site, like that of Antonio Mannini in 1411, involve only a detailed description of the paperwork, interviews, and permissions involved in gaining admission.

St. Patrick's Purgatory (Tractatus de Purgatorio Sancti Patricii)

Owein's vision, however, does describe his experience of the purgatory itself. His visit occurs just at the time when the concept of purgatory was becoming set as a doctrine in the Christian church. One of the important characteristics of this work, which distinguishes it from most of the other visions included here is the presumption of the actual physical and corporeal nature of the experience of the knight Owein whom we follow through the Purgatory. As in *St. Brendan's Voyage,* there is no separation from the body, and all that he experiences he is assumed to experience corporally. Although other visions, like Tundale's, approach the otherworld with the same attention to physical and corporeal details, in other cases the soul of the visionary is actually separated from the body.

A similarity might be pointed out between this work and *Charles the Fat's Vision.* In both cases the question of war plays a significant part. In Charles' vision the punishments he sees are related strictly to participation in and condoning of war. In this work the motivation for the penance undertaken by Owein is his own participation, as a knight of King Stephen (d. 1154), in a life of plunder and violence. He enters the Purgatory to begin the purgation that will continue when he returns from the Purgatory, and even in the afterlife, unless he has managed to cleanse himself completely.

Shortly after Owein descends into St. Patrick's Purgatory, he enters a hall enclosed by pillars where he meets fifteen men. Although he is not guided by these, he is advised by one of them to say the name of "Jesus" whenever things are going awry, and he is warned not to accept any offers to return back to the cave before completing the journey through the Purgatory. The otherworld begins with a series of plains where souls are tortured. Owein is treated badly by the demons he meets in purgatory, but he always remembers to invoke the name of Jesus, and he also refuses the numerous offers to lead him back to the entrance.

In addition to the plains of tortured, there is also a wheel of red-hot nails, a house of boiling cauldrons, a mountain swept by a whirlwind, a stinking and cold river, a pit that some demons claim is the mouth of hell, and a narrow and slippery bridge. These trials are not associated with individual sins but are general punishments.

Finally Owein arrives at an antechamber to heaven, which is described in terms of walls and gates of precious stones and metals, music, and wonderful vegetation. He is shown the gate of heaven and then refreshed with celestial food. Despite his own misgivings about his ability to reform, he is sent back to the entrance past all the demons who can no longer hurt him.

Owein meets no former acquaintances on his journey through purgatory. As a result of his experience he repents further of his evil life, makes a pilgrimage to the Holy Land, and finally devotes the rest of his life to helping a monastic community in Ireland. His companion in establishing this community, Gilbert, writes down the story and relates it to Hugh of Saltry who wrote down the authoritative version.

The Vision of William Staunton

A Middle English vision at St. Patrick's Purgatory of purgatory and the earthly paradise, which is said to have occurred on the first Friday after the feast of the Exaltation of the Cross in 1409. William is guided by St. John of Bridlyngton and St. Ive (of Quitike). The visionary does not suffer much, but he is constantly in danger of punishments fitted to sins. There is a discussion on the efficacy of prayer and almsgiving to relieve purgatorial suffering. Among those he meets is his sister and her lover, whose marriage he opposed. The visionary witnesses the trial of a prioress found guilty of wearing expensive decorations. (See **463**.)

The Vision of Louis of France (Visio Ludovici de Francia)

This French vision dates from 1358 and is also known as the *Vision of Louis de Sur* or *Louis d'Auxerre*. It follows much the same format as other visions from St. Patrick's Purgatory, with the particular details that Louis sees a king who is tortured but has relief for certain periods because of his generosity in alms. See Strecker (**476**) and Voigt (**480**).

The following visions are much the same except for those met in the otherworld and the messages they bring back.

Raymond de Perehlos (1397 visit)

Laurence Rathold (1411)

George, Knight of Hungary (mid fourteenth century, Provencal origin, also known as **George Grissophan** [1353], who came as a penitent. This version of the legend provides the first eyewitness account of the topography of Lough Derg.)

Laurent de Paszatho (Jacobus Yonge. *Le Pélerinage de Laurent de Paszatho au Purgatorie de S. Patrice.* 1908. Not seen.)

Bibliographies
442   BHL 2:938–24; Suppl. 244–46; New Suppl. 685–89.

Sources
443   Atkinson Jenkins, Thomas. *"Espurgatoire Seint Patriz" of Marie de France: An Old-French Poem of the Twelfth Century.* Philadelphia: Ferris, 1894; rpt. Chicago, Il.: University of Chicago Press, 1903; Geneva: Slatkine, 1974; also in *Chicago University Decennial Publications,* ser. 1, 7 (1903): 233–327.

Critical edition of Anglo-Norman text. Introduction
discusses the legend, Marie's Latin original and her
dialect, the order of Marie's works, and the date, language
and mss of the *Espurgatoire*. Review by G. Paris,
Romania 24 (1895): 290–95.

444   Bertolini, Lucia. "Per una della leggende 'che illustrano la
        Divina Commedia.'" *Studi Danteschi* 53 (1981): 69–
        128.

An annotated critical edition of an Italian *Purgatorio
di San Patrizio* based on three mss with an introduction
on the mss and editorial method.

445   Brunet, Gustave, ed. *Le Voyage du pays sainct Patrix,
        auquel lieu on voit les peines du purgatoire et aussi
        les joyes de Paradis.* Geneva: J. Gay, 1867.

Not seen. (B.N. Paris Rés. D. 63257.) Edition of
Latin text based on 102 examples.

446   Caerwyn Williams, J. E. "Welsh Versions of the
        Purgatorium S. Patricii." *Studia Celtica* 8–9 (1973–
        74): 121–94.

Introduction provides background on otherworld
vision literature, on St. Patrick's Purgatory, its mss, and
editions; lists mss containing Welsh versions of the
Tractatus; provides a comparison of the various Welsh
texts and presents a critical edition based on ms
Llanstephan 27 with variants from Peniarth 5 and
Llanstephan 4 with facing Latin from London, B.L. Royal
13 B. viii.

447   Curley, Michael, ed. *Saint Patrick's Purgatory. A Poem by Marie de France.* Binghampton, N.Y.: Medieval and Renaissance Texts and Studies, forthcoming.

         Not seen. An edition of the French text from the edition by Warnke (**481**) with a facing English translation and an introduction discussing the date, historical and literary background, and relationship between this work and Marie's other works. Bibliography and notes.

448   Delehaye, Hippolytus, ed. "La Pèlerinage de Laurent de Paszthou au Purgatoire de S. Patrice." AB 27 (1908): 35–60.

         Presents an edition of the Latin text found in London, B.L. Royal 10.B.ix. Introduction discusses sixteen other visitors to the Purgatory who left accounts. Delehaye has published this text in an attempt to insure that a knowledge of these visions is not lacking when we consider the significance of St. Patrick.

449   Easting, R. B., ed. "An Edition of *Owain Miles* and other Middle English Texts Concerning St. Patrick's Purgatory." P.Phil. Diss.: Oxford University, 1976.

         Not seen. Prints in parallel: B.L. Royal 17.B.xlii; B.L. Add. Ms 34,194; B.L., Cotton Caligula A.ii; Yale Ms 365 (Book of Brome).

450   ———. "Peter of Cornwall's Account of St. Patrick's Purgatory." AB 97 (1979): 397–416.

         Edition of the Latin text (c. 1200) from Lambeth Palace Library Ms. 51 with an introduction on this vision by an unnamed knight and its relationship to Owein's vision. Includes description of ms.

451 ———, ed. *St. Patrick's Purgatory.* Early English Text
Society 298. Oxford: Oxford University Press, 1991.

Critical edition of two versions of the Middle English
"Owayne Miles," the Middle English *Vision of William
Staunton,* and the Latin *Tractatus.* Introduction on St.
Patrick's Purgatory, mss, language, previous editions,
and the texts. Includes select bibliography and glossary.

452 Endepols, H. J. E. *Die Hijstoirie van Sunte Patricus'
Vegevuer naar een Berlisjnsch Handschrift. Van alle
tijden* 8. Groningen: Wolters, 1919.

Annotated diplomatic edition of Dutch text with
translation into modern Dutch.

453 Frati, Ludovico, ed. "Il Purgatorio di S. Patrizio secondo
Stefano di Bourbon e Umberto da Romans."
Giornale Storico della Letteratura Italiana 8 (1886):
140–79.

Discusses this version of *St. P's P* concluding that it
does not belong to the body of literature on which Dante
relied.

454 ———. "Tradizioni Storiche del Purgatorio di San
Patrizio." *Giornale Storico della Letteratura Italiana*
17 (1891): 46–79.

Discusses the importance and popularity of this
legend and lists Latin, French, Provençal, English,
Spanish, Italian, and Swedish versions with editions.

455 Gardiner, see **32**, pp. 135–48.

Includes English translation of the *Tractatus* with notes and bibliography.

456   Grion, Giusto. "Il pozzo di San Patrizio." *Il Propugnatore* 3 (1870): 67–149.

Edition of the Venetian text of the Owein legend with introduction.

457   Hammerich, L. L., ed. *Visiones Georgii: Visiones quas in Purgatorio Sancti Patricii vidit Georgius Miles de Ungaria, A.D. MCCCLIII.* Copenhagen: Høst, 1931.

Critical edition of Latin text of the *Vision of George Grissophan* or George of Hungary. Introduction on mss.

458   ———, ed. "Le pelerinage de Louis d'Auxerre au Purgatoire de S. Patrice. *Romania* 5:118ff.

Not seen. Edition of French text.

459   Holdsworth, see **39**.

Presents Latin texts with brief introduction to Lambeth Palace 51,   Peter of Cornwall's *Liber revelationum,* which includes a version of *St. Patrick's Purgatory.*

460   Horstmann, see **164**, pp. 199–220.

Edition of Middle English text based on Laud 108, Bodley 186 and 692, Egerton 1993. (Reprinted from Horstmann, *Altenglische Legenden* Paderborn, 1875.)

461   Jeanroy, A., and A. Vignaux. *Voyage au Purgatoire de St. Patrice: Visions de Tindal et de St. Paul: textes*

languedociens du quinzième siècle. Bibliothèque
méridonale, ser. 1, vol. 8. Toulouse: E. Privat, 1903;
rpt. New York: Johnson Reprint, 1971.

Raimon de Perehlos version. Includes an introduction
to the ms (Toulouse B.M. 894) and previous editions of
it, a discussion of the language, a glossary, and an index
of names. It is based on H. of Sawtry's (Saltry) story of
Knight Owein but here Raimon de Perehlos tells it as if
he himself made the visit to the purgatory. Provides
detailed information on this fourteenth-century author.

462   Kölbing, Eugen. "Zwei mittelenglische Bearbeitungen
der Sage von St. Patrik's Purgatorium." *Englische
Studien* 1 (1877): 57–121.

Annotated diplomatic edition of the Middle English
Purgatorium Sancti Patricii (pp. 98–113) and *Owein
Miles* (113–21). Detailed introduction discusses mss,
editions; compares different versions in effort to elucidate
history of these texts. Review with corrections to text by
J. Zupitza in *Zeitschrift für Deutsches Archivgescgichte*
22 n.f.(10) (1878): 248–51. Kolbing issued a list of
revised readings in *Englische Studien* 7 (1884): 181–82.
See Easting (**451**), pp. xl–xli.

463   Krapp, George Philip. *The Legend of Saint Patrick's
Purgatory: Its Later Literary History.* Baltimore:
John Murphy, 1900.

Study of the later history of the legend of St. Patrick's
Purgatory with a critical edition of the Middle English
Vision of William Staunton based on B.L. Royal 17.B.
xliii (primary text) and B.L. Add. 34,193 (pp. 35–77
including introduction and summary). Discusses the
diffusion of the legend, especially in Spain (the history of

Luis Enius), France, and Great Britain, and provides an introduction to the text.

464   Mall, Ed. "Zur Geschichte der Legende vom Purgatorium des heil. Patricius." *Romanische Forschungen* 6 (1891): 139–97.

In a discussion of the background of Marie de France's version of this work, this article presents a comparison of editions of two Latin texts: John Colgan's *Triadis Thaumaturgae...acta* (Louvain, 1647) and Bamberg MS E.VII.50, with variants from B.L. Arundel 292.

465   Marchand, see **97**, pp. viii–xiii, xxvi–xxx, 79–115.

French translation of the *Tractatus* of H. of Sawtry (Saltry). Provides a brief introduction and bibliography.

466   Matthew Paris. *Chronica maioribus.* Ed. by H. R. Luard. 2 vols. London: P. unk., 1874, 192–203, anno 1153; 212–14, anno 1156.

Not seen.

467   Meyer, Paul. "Légendes Hagiographiques en Français." *Histoire littéraire de la France.* Paris: Imprimerie Nationale, 1906, 33: 371–72, 378–458.

Lists the manuscripts and editions of the seven French verse versions of H. of Sawtry's (Saltry) *St. Patrick's Purgatory.* Six are in octosyllabic verse; two were composed in France, the rest in England. Includes the versions attributed to Marie de France (Paris B.N. Fr. 25407); the version by Beroul (Cheltenham, Phillipps 4156, Tours 948); the version by Gaufroi de Paris (Paris

B.N. Fr. 1526); and four anonymous versions found in mss in the British Library (Cotton Domit. A. iv; Harley 273, Lansdowne 383), at Cambridge (Univ. Ee.6.11); and in Paris (B.N. Fr. 2198). Discussion of mss of prose versions is scattered through pp. 378–458.

468   Mörner, Marianne, ed. *Le Purgatoire de Saint Patrice par Bérol.* Lund: P. Lindstedt, 1917.

Not seen.

469   ———. *Le Purgatoire de Saint Patrice du manuscrit de la Bibl. Nat. fonds fr. 25545.* Lund Universitets Arsskrift, ser. 1, vol. 16, no. 4. Lund: Gleerup, 1920.

Diplomatic edition of French verse version with notes and glossary. Introduction discusses the relationship between the French poem and the Latin legend; the ms; versification and language and origin and date of the poem. Anonymous work from east of France, possibly Champagne, dating from the last years of the thirteenth century.

470   PL 180:973–1004.

Unannotated Latin edition of *Tractatus de Purgatorio Sancti Patricii Hibernorumapostoli.* Based on Thomas of Messingham, *Florilegium insulae sanctorum, seu vitae et acta sanctorum Hiberniae* (Paris: 1624, in quarto). Includes "prologus Henricii Salteriensis in purgatorium patricii."

471   Picard, Jean-Michel, and Yolande de Pontfarcy. *Saint Patrick's Purgatory: A Twelfth Century Tale of a Journey to the Otherworld.* Dublin: Four Courts Press, 1985.

Brief introduction to the history of Lough Derg mentioning some of the more famous visitors and some of the better studies. Discusses the authorship and date; folk, historical, literary and clerical sources. Text is an English translation of the Latin *Tractatus*. Select bibliography, including section on Lough Derg itself.

472   Roger of Wendover, see **332**, 2:256–71.

Diplomatic edition of Latin text of Owein legend with historical annotations. (See also 2:284–86.)

473   Roger of Wendover, see **333**, 1:510–22.

English translation of the Knight Owein legend based on the Coxe edition (**332**). Preface discusses Roger, the nature of his work and his sources. (See also 1:530–31 note.)

474   Smith, Lucy Toulmin. "St. Patrick's Purgatory, and the Knight Sir Owne." *Englische Studien* 9 (1886): 1–12.

Diplomatic edition of text of Middle English *Owayne Miles* with introduction.

475   ———. *A Common-place Book of the Fifteenth Century.* London and Norwich: p. unk., 1886, 80–106.

Not seen. Revised text of **474** reprinted with introduction.

476   Strecker. *Visio Ludovici de Francis.* Leipzig: P. unk., 1924.

Not seen. Edition of *Vision of Louis of France.*

477 Verdeyen, R., and J. Endepols. *Tondalus' Visionen en St. Patricus' Vagevuur.* Ghent: Siffer/Koninklijke Vlaamsche Academie, 1914–17, 2:177–318

Study by Endepols of the Purgatory of St. Patrick with a list of mss in vol. 1. Annotated critical edition of Middle Dutch text in vol. 2.

478 Villari, see **72**, *Antiche Leggende* 51–76, *Annali* 103–28.

Italian edition based on Florence, B.N. Palatini 93 compared with B.N. Cod. Magl., Conv. Sopp. 676, G.3.

479 Vising, Johan. *Le purgatoire de saint Patrice: des manuscrits harleien 273 et fonds francais 2198.* Goteborg Hogskolas Arsskrift vol. 21, no. 3, 1916; rpt. Geneva: Slatkine Reprints, 1974.

Introduction on texts and mss, versification, the language of the author of the Harley ms, and the date of the poem. Critical edition of the French verse version. Includes extensive commentary and glossary.

480 Voigt, Max. *Beiträge zur Geschichte der Visionen-literatur im Mittelalter.* Leipzig: Mayer & Müller, 1924; rpt. New York: Johnson Reprint, 1967.

Introduction on the history of pilgrimages, continental pilgrims to St. Patrick's Purgatory in Ireland, including George of Hungary or George Grissophan with a list of Latin mss; a summary of George's vision, a discussion of the work and author, the German adaptation (including a list of mss), and the literary successor (Ludovicus de Francia), with a critical edition of the Latin text. (226–45). Originally appeared in *Palestra* 16.

481   Warnke, Karl, ed. *Das Buch vom Espurgatoire S.
       Patrice der Marie de France und seine Quelle.*
       Bibliotheca normannica 9. Halle/Saale: M. Niemeyer,
       1938.

       Critical edition with manuscript variants of Latin text
       (two versions in parallel columns) of the *Tractatus* of H.
       of Sawtry (Saltrey) with the French translation on the
       opposite page. The introduction discusses the legend, the
       mss, the narrative, the growth and development of the
       text, its style and grammar, as well as other versions of
       the legend.

482   Waterhouse, Gilbert, ed. "Another Early German
       Account of St. Patrick's Purgatory." *Hermathena* 23
       (1933): 114–16.

       Provides a very brief introduction and translation into
       English of a fifteenth-century version found in Trinity
       College Library, Dublin (Press A, 7.19) and a pamphlet
       from the Lough Fea collection in the same library. This
       work is based on chapter one of H. of Sawtry (Saltry),
       concerning the entry into the Purgatory, and ending with
       the story of a man who didn't believe in the Purgatory
       and was found dead (and black as coal) with a note in his
       hand saying that he had seen purgatory and hell and they
       were awful.

483   Zanden, Cornelis M. Van der, ed. *Étude sur le purgatoire
       de Saint Patrice, accompagnée du texte latin
       d'Utrecht et du texte anglo-normand de Cambridge.*
       Amsterdam: H. J. Paris, 1927.

       Includes Latin text based on one ms from Utrecht
       with a description of mss and consideration of other mss;
       Anglo-Norman text based on two mss, notes on the

language and versification, description of mss and consideration of other French versions. Appendix includes text of Arundel 292 in Latin. Glossary.

Studies
484   Ancona, see **3**, pp. 59–63.

Treats the antecedents of Dante in general and gives some particular attention to the Paul, Brendan, Tundale, Patrick, and Alberic visions. He does not make firm connections between these and the *Divine Comedy*, but indicates a general milieu of vision literature, which does not detract from Dante's originality.

485   Baring-Gould, Sabine. *Curious Myths of the Middle Ages.* Intro. by Leslie Shepard. New Hyde Park, N.Y.: University Books, 1967, 230–49; abridged ed., ed. with intro. by Edward Hardy, New York: Oxford University Press, 1978, 85–87.

Very cursory discussion of visits by Fortunatus, Knight Owein, and William Staunton, of references to the Purgatory in chronicles, etc., of the history of the site, and of ancient and celtic influences on the development of the Purgatory legend. Includes brief bibliography.

486   Bieler, Ludwig. "St. Patrick's Purgatory: Contributions towards an Historical Topography." *The Irish Ecclesiastical Record* 93 (1960): 137–44.

Examines sometimes contradictory accounts of the purgatory to determine the location and concludes that it was on Station Island in Lough Derg, not Saints Island; that the actual site on the island was the same in all accounts except perhaps for the descent into the pit by the canon of Eymsteade (1494). Discusses how the site was turned from a place of individual penitence to organized pilgrimage.

487   Boas, see **9**, pp. 54–74.

Study of "primitivism" which examines the idea of the earthly paradise using several examples but in particular the *Vision of Tundale, St. Patrick's Purgatory*, and *St. Brendan's Voyage*.

488   Curtayne, Alice. *Lough Derg: St. Patrick's Purgatory*. London and Dublin: Burns, Oates & Washbourne, 1945.

A history of Lough Derg for the modern pilgrim, which includes a chapter (pp. 27–40) on the Owein legend.

489   Degli Innocenti, Mario. "Radazioni italiane del *Purgatorio di S. Patrizio.*" *Italia, medioevale e umanistica* 27 (1984): 81–120.

A study of the relationships of the various Italian versions of *St. P.'s P.* (Tuscan, Lombard, Venetian) to each other, to the Latin text, and to other vernacular versions.

490   Dixon, V. F. "Saint Patrick of Ireland and the Dramatists of Golden Age Spain." *Hermathena* 121 (1976): 142–58.

Focuses on Juan Pérez de Mantalbán's *Vida y purgatorio de San Patricio* and the two plays: *El mayor prodigio* attributed to Lope de Vada and *El purgatorio de San Patricio* by Calderon, and discusses the development of the legend in these works.

491   Easting, Robert. "The Date and Dedication of the
       Tractatus de Purgatorio Sancti Patricii." Speculum
       53 (1978): 778–83.

       Refutes Locke's arguments (**512**), and claims that the
       dedicatee was Hugh of Wardon and not Henry of
       Wardon, and proposes that the work was written most
       likely c. 1179–81.

492   ———. "Owein at St. Patrick's Purgatory." *Medium
       Aevum* 55, 2 (1986): 159–75.

       Discusses the character of Owein and his possible
       origins in mythology – but prefers to assume that he was
       a historical character; the date of the visit, which he places
       in 1146/7, based on the dates connected with the
       monastery he helped build at Baltinglass; Owein's trip to
       the Holy Land (as a pilgrim, not a crusader); and the
       ultimate fate of Owein – probably as a monk at
       Baltinglass.

493   ———. "Purgatory and the Earthly Paradise in the
       *Tractatus de Purgatorio Sancti Patricii." Cîteaux:
       Commentarii Cistercienses* 37 (1986): 23–48.

       Not seen.

494   ———. "The Middle English 'Hearne Fragment' of *St.
       Patrick's Purgatory." Notes and Queries* 35 (1988):
       436–37.

       Connects this fragment with B.L. Harley 4012 and
       thus revises Forster's (**29**) assessment of the number of
       Middle English versions (four rather than six).

495   ———. "Some Antedatings and Early Usages from the Auchinleck *Owayne Miles."* In *Sentences for Alan Ward.* Edited by D. M. Reeks. Southampton: Bosphorus Books, 1988, 167–74.

Concludes from ms evidence that the Auchinlech *Owayne Miles* is the most romantic and individual of the many medieval vernacular translations of the Owayne story.

496   ———. "The South English Legendary 'St. Patrick' as Translation." *Leeds Studies in English* 21 (1990): 119–40.

Not seen.

497   ———. "Middle English Translations of the *Tractatus de Purgatorio Sancti Patricii."* In *The Medieval Translator II.* Edited by Roger Ellis. London: University of London, 1991, 151–74.

Discusses the Middle English translations from Latin and the tendencies to translate an attitude and manner: movement from narrative, meditative, eschatologically theoretical to the romance and drama of personal heroism, which is possible because Owayne is a knight and the St. Patrick's Purgatory an actual place.

498   Eckleben, Selmar. *Die älteste Schilderung vom Fegefeuer das heiligen Patricius: Eine litterarische Untersuchung.* Halle: M. Niemeyer, 1885.

Study of the merit of the legend, its place in the legend literature, and the origin of the Latin version. Krapp (**463**) notes that "the author's final conclusion is that the legend in its origin was a mere monkish fabrication for mercenary purpose."

499   Esposito, E. "Notes on Latin Learning and Literature in Medieval Ireland." *Hermathena* 50(1937): 162–67.

Enumerates seventy Latin mss of the *Purgatory,* plus the mss of four other narratives associated with this location: George Grissophan, Taddeus de Gualandis of Pisa, and Raimon de Perehlos.

500   Félice, Philippe de. *L'Autre Monde: Mythes et Légendes: Le Purgatoire de saint Patrice.* Paris: Champion, 1906.

Not seen, but called "a well-documented study on the history of pilgrimage and on the texts" (Marchand **97**).

501   Foster, see **29**, 2:453–55, 646–48.

Description and bibliography of the Middle English St. Patrick's Purgatory. (See **494**.)

502   Foulet, Lucien. "Marie de France et la Légende du Purgatoire de Saint Patrice." *Romanische Forschungen* 22 (1908): 599–627.

A brief study of this work in comparison with the Latin original.

503   Gaidoz, H. "Pilgrimage of the Hungarian Nobleman to St. Patrick's Purgatory." *Revue Celtique* 2 (1872): 482–84.

Brief note on George, the Hungarian Knight's vision with a discussion of the text and mss.

504   Garcia Solalinde, Antonio. *La primera versión española de "El purgatorio de San Patricio" y la difusión de esta leyanda en España.* Madrid: Hernando, 1924.

Discusses the birth of the legend, its spread through Europe, and the first Spanish text, presenting a diplomatic edition of it, an analysis of the Latin original, a comparison of the Spanish text with the *Tractatus,* and a study of the author, date and language of the Spanish text.

505   Hammerich, L. L. "Studies of Visiones Georgii." *Classica et medievalia. Revue danoise de philologie et d'histoire* 1 (1938): 95–118, 2(1939): 190–220.

Not seen.

506   Kenney, see **90**, pp. 354–56.

Brief description with bibliography to 1929.

507   Le Goff, Jacques. "Les Gestes du purgatoire." In *L'Art des confins. Melanges offerts à Maurice de Gandillac.* Ed. by Annie Cazenave and Jean-Francois Lyotard. Paris: Presses Universitaires de France, 1985, 457–64.

Examines the system of gestures in relation to the space of purgatory as revealed in *St. Patrick's Purgatory,* discussing the idea of the gesturing and the gestured at (or those who act as opposed to those acted upon), and relating it to the new idea of the purgation in the Christian afterlife.

508   Leslie, Shane, ed. *The Story of St. Patrick's Purgatory.*
       St. Louis and London: Herder, 1917.

       Not seen.

509   ———. *Saint Patrick's Purgatory: A Record from
       History and Literature.* London: Burns, Oates &
       Washbourne, 1932.

       A collection of extracts and documents with their
       sources to illustrate the history of St. Patrick's Purgatory
       from the Middle Ages to the early twentieth century.
       Makes many unusual documents available but does not
       present a complete version of any of the major literary
       texts.

510   ———. "St. Patrick's Purgatory." *The Script of Jonathan
       Swift and Other Essays.* Philadelphia: University of
       Pennsylvania Press, 1935, 57–70.

       Attempts to trace the passing of folklore into
       medieval legend and the crystalization of both in the
       religious tradition of the Irish Celts with a very general
       essay on the legend of Lough Derg and its passing into
       written text.

511   ———. *Saint Patrick's Purgatory.* Monaghan, Ireland: P.
       unk., 1961.

       Not seen.

512   Locke, F. W. "A New Date for the Composition of the
       Tractatus de Purgatorio Sancti Patricii." Speculum
       40 (1965): 641–46.

Argues for dating the *Tractatus* between 1208 and 8 April 1215 based on various pieces of evidence but hinging on the period of Henry's rule over St. Mary de Sartris or Warden, to whom, he claims, this work is dedicated. (See **491**.)

513   Lyle, E. B. "The Visions of St. Patrick's Purgatory, Thomas of Erceldoune, Thomas the Rhymer, and the Demon Lovers." *Neuphilologische Mittelungen* 72 (1972): 716–22.

Not seen.

514   McAlindon, T. "Comedy and Terror in Middle English Literature: The Diabolical Game." *Modern Language Review* 60/3 (1965): 323–32.

In the context of Middle English literature in general, and particularly drama, author discusses the playful devils found in *St. P's P.* (esp. pp. 326–28).

515   MacBride, P. "St. Patrick's Purgatory in Spanish Literature." *Studies: An Irish Quarterly* 25 (1936): 277–91.

An overview of the Patrick story in Spanish literature including the discovery of the ms. from which Philip O'Sullevan Beare took his account of the voyage of Perehlos to Lough Derg in 1397.

516   Mac Tréinfhir, Noel. "The Todi Fresco and St. Patrick's Purgatory, Lough Derg." *Clogher Record* 12 (1986): 141–58.

Not seen.

517   Mahaffy, John Pentland. "Two Early Tours of Ireland."
        Hermathena no. 40, vol. 18 (1919): 1–16.

        This work is more concerned with what occurs
        previous to the entry into the Purgatory. Includes a
        translation of a portion of the Perehlos work (see **461**)
        and the complete text of a letter of Francesco Chiericati,
        papal nuncio at the court of Henry VIII, to Isabella
        D'Este referring to the Purgatory, but not describing the
        actual experience in the Purgatory. The introduction hints
        at a prototype for the *Purgatory* in Greek mystery
        initiations, such as the Eleusinian mysteries and the cave
        of Trophonius, but Mahaffy does not persue this idea.

518   Miquel y Planas, Ramón. *Influencia del "Purgatorio de
        sant Patrici" en la llegenda de Don Juan.* Barcelona:
        Casa provencial de caritat, 1914.

        A brief work on the influence of the Perehlos version
        on the Don Juan legend in Spain. Includes extensive
        notes.

519   O'Connor, Daniel. *St. Patrick's Purgatory, Lough Derg.*
        Rev. ed. Dublin: Duffy, and New York: Benziger
        Bros., 1895, 1903, 1910. (Published as *Lough Derg
        and Its Pilgrims.* Dublin: Joseph Dollard, 1879.)

        A popular history of Lough Derg, its history,
        legends, antiquities, topography, surroundings, and
        pilgrims.

520   Pinkerton, W. "St. Patrick's Purgatory." *Ulster Journal
        of Archaeology* 4 (1856): 40–52, 101–17, 222–38.

Discusses the legendary backgrounds to St. Patrick's Purgatory and the legends of Owein, Raymond of Perehlos, and William Staunton.

521   Pontfarcy, Y. de. *"Le Tractatus de Purgatorio Sancti Patricii* de H. de Saltrey: sa date et ses sources." *Pertitia: Journal of the Medieval Academy of Ireland* 3 (1984): 460–80.

Examination of the date and sources, concluding that "the story of Owein was transmitted to the monk H. de Saltry, who, on the request of his abbot H. de Sartis, wrote the first version of the story in 1184, which he expanded a little later (1186–88), assuring by the popularity of his work, the European fame of the Purgatory." Among other sources mentions Adamnán, Laisren, Gregory the Great, and Paul.

522   Ringger, Kurt. "Die Altfranzösischen Verspurgatorien." *Zeitschrift für Romanische Philologie* 88 (1972): 389–402.

Examines the question of authorship. Was the author, indeed, Marie de France, an identification accepted by so many scholars?

523   Rockelein, see **62**.

Combines psychological and ethnological approaches in a study of Otloh of Emmeran with particular reference to the "collective" visions of Gottschalk, Thurkill, Tundale, and Owein (*St. Patrick's Purgatory*).

524   Ryan, John. "Saint Patrick's Purgatory." *Studies* 21 (1932): 443–60.

Discusses this work in the context of pilgrimage, as well as evidence regarding its location and the nature of the visions there.

525   ———. "St. Patrick's Purgatory, Lough Derg." In *Clogher Record Album*. Edited by Joseph A. Duffy. Monaghan: P. unk., 1975, 12–26.

Not seen.

526   Seymour, St. John Drelincourt. *St. Patrick's Purgatory: A Medieval Pilgrimage in Ireland*. Dundalk: W. Tempest, 1918.

Gives a brief account of the history of Lough Derg, relates at some length the visions seen by certain pilgrims, deals with the literature that arose and the effect this had on the literary life of Europe, and finally discusses the history of the cave and the monastery from the suppression at the end of the fifteenth century to the present. A well-annotated study for the general reader. Covers David of Würzburg, Joscelin, Giraldus Cambrensis, H. of Sawtry (Saltry), George Grissophan, Raymond de Perehlos, William of Staunton, Antonio Mannini and Laurence Rathold de Pasztho.

527   Shields, H.E. "An Old French Book of Legends and its Apocalypic Background." Ph.D. Diss.: Trinity College, Dublin, 1967, pp. 336–62, and appendix 1.

Not seen.

528   Stanford, M.A. *"The Sumner's Tale* and *St. Patrick's Purgatory." Journal of English and Germanic Philology* 19 (1920): 377–81.

On Chaucer's description of purgatory and its probable reliance on the *St. Patrick's Purgatory* in the South English Legendary.

529   Vinton, Frederick. "*St. Patrick's Purgatory* and the *Inferno* of Dante." *Bibla Sacra* 30 (1873): 275–400.

Not seen.

530   Ward, see **306**, 2 (1893): 435–92, 748.

Includes descriptions of Latin mss: Royal 13 B. viii, Arundel 292, Cotton Nero A. vii, Royal 8 C. xiv, Harley 261, Harley 3776, Harley 103, Royal 9 A. xiv, Cotton Vesp. A. vi., Cotton Tiberius E. i., Harley 3846, Egerton 1117, Add. 33,957, Harley 912; French mss: Cotton Domit. A. iv., Harley 273, Lansdowne 383, Add. 6524; English mss: Egerton 1993, Cotton Julius D. ix., Add. 10,301, Cotton Caligula A. ii., Royal 17 B. xliii, Add. 34,193; and Latin mss: Royal 10 B. ix, and Harley 2851.

531   Warnke, Karl, ed. "Die Vorlage des Espurgatorie St. Patriz der Marie de France." *Philologische Studien Karl Voretzsch zum 60 Geburstage.* Halle/Saale: Max Niemeyer, 1927.

Not seen.

532   Waterhouse, G. "An Early German Account of St. Patrick's Purgatory." *Modern Language Review* 18 (1923): 317–22.

Edition of 90-line fragment of fifteenth-century German text, from Trinity College Dublin, with remarks concluding that the German is an indirect not a direct translation from the Latin.

533 ———. "St. Patrick's Purgatoy: A German Account."
Hermathena 20 (1930): 30–51.

On dating the *Tractatus.*

534 Wright, Thomas. *St. Patrick's Purgatory: An Essay on
the Legends of Purgatory, Hell and Paradise
Current during the Middle Ages.* London: John
Russell Smith, 1844.

Antipapist study of visions as superstition with *St.
Ps'P* as a focal point. Wright discusses the history of
medieval visions of purgatory, heaven, and hell (often
mentioning mss) – Furseus, Paul, Drythelm, Charles the
Fat, the Boy William, Tundale, the Monk of Eynsham,
Thurkill, etc., generally recounting the important features
of the vision, dealing with them chronologically, right
down to the modern period. Sees all this literature as a
plot by the Catholic priesthood to keep the Catholic
peasantry under control. Equates belief with superstition.
Makes some attempt to trace ideas on heaven and hell or
"how these strange foreign takes affected sensible Anglo-
Saxon minds."

535 Zaleski, Carol. "*St. Patrick's Purgatory:* Pilgrimage
Motifs in a Medieval Otherworld Vision." *Journal of
the History of Ideas* 46 (1985) 467–85.

Reviews the background of Lough Derg; and
analyzes the legend of the Knight Owein in relation to
issues of pilgrimage, penance and eschatology.

536 Zanden, Cornelius M. Van der. "Auteur d'un manuscrit
latin du *Purgatoire de Saint Patrice* de la
Bibliothèque de l'Université d'Utrecht."
Neophilologus 10 (1925): 243–49.

Postulates that this ms (Utrecht 173) presents a possible primitive version of the text.

537   ———. "Un chapitre intéressant de la 'Topographia Hibernica' et le "Tractatus de Purgatorio sancti Patricii.'" *Neophilologus* 12 (1927): 132–37.

Discusses the interpolation of the *Purgatorio* into Giraldus Cambrensis' *Topographia* in the Utrecht ms (Univ. Bibl. 173) and the reasons for it.

THE VISION OF ST. PAUL

The Latin Vision of St. Paul was strongly influenced by Greek ideas of the afterlife, as included in the third-century Greek version of the vision, the *Apocalypse of Paul.* The starting point of the legend is the *raptus* of Paul (2 Corinthians 12.1–5). It was based initially on the apocalypses of Peter, Zephaniah, and Elias, and the *Book of Enoch*. It dates from the late fourth century. This vision was a popular work with versions in almost every European language, including Italian, Provencal, Old French, Danish, and Anglo-Saxon and Middle English, German, and Anglo-Norman, with earlier versions in Syriac, Coptic, and Ethiopic. From the Latin text was made a French version by Adam de Ros and thence translations into various European tongues. There are eleven Latin redactions with over fifty extant mss. Vernacular versions derive mostly from Redaction IV. The work has a great influence of later visions and is often referred to.

The vision begins with the discovery of a sealed lead box under Paul's house in Tarsus in 388 CE. The box contains the story of Paul being taken up bodily into heaven. An unusual feature of this vision is its opening in which Paul witnesses the sun, moon and stars, sea, waters, and earth, all asking the Lord to let them destroy, in one way or another, the inhabitants of the earth because of their dreadful behavior.

Paul is introduced to the guardian angels who recount the deeds of their charges before God. Then Paul is taken up in the spirit to the Place of the Righteous where he sees the Firmaments and the Powers and the evil and good angels. Paul is also shown what happens when both evil and good souls departs from the body and how their angels present them before God.

Paul witnesses the death of a man, the struggle to take the soul from the body, the judgment of the soul and its condemnation to hell.

179

Paul's guide is Michael the Archangel., who shows Paul hell, where people are punished according to their sins, then shows him heaven and finally returns him to earth.

This vision presents a fairly detailed description of three heavens with the third being a city, similar to the apocalyptic Heavenly Jerusalem, with walls, twelve gates, and four rivers. In heaven Paul meets many Hebrew prophets and has a conversation with Enoch, which he is not allowed to reveal.

In his vision of hell Paul sees the usual range of sinners, and, in addition, unworthy priests, bishops, deacons, and lectors. The punishments in hell generally include immersion in a river of fire up to various parts of the body, but there are also worms and dragons that devour the sinners, and vile pits into which the sinners are thrown. St. Paul witnesses these scenes but does not suffer any pains. This vision results in the Lord granting the souls, at the request of Paul, Michael, and the angels, a day without torments. Such interest in the relief of sinners becomes an increasingly important feature of visions of heaven and hell.

Paul's vision presents the first instance of the judgment of individual souls at their death. It is also worth noting that the church and the levels of the hierarchy in the church had developed to a point where different classes of male clerics were mentioned in connection with their specific roles and not fulfilling them properly.

Bibliographies
538   BHL 2:953–55; Suppl. 248–49; New Suppl. 696–700.

539   Silverstein, see **568**, pp, 219–29.

Sources
540   Appel, Carl Ludwig Ernst, ed. *Provenzalische Chrestomathie.* Leipzig: O.R. Reisland, 1895, 177–79.

Critical edition of Provencal version based on one ms and Bartsch edition (**541**).

541   Bartsch, Karl Friederich, ed. *Denkmæler der provenzalischen Literatur.* Stuttgart: Literarischer verien Bibliothek, 1856, 310–15.

Diplomatic edition of Provencal version.

542   Brandes, Herman, ed. *Visio Sancti Pauli; ein Beiträg zur Visionsliteratur mit einen deutschen und zwei lateinischen Texten.* Gesellschaft für deutsche Philologie. Festschrift 5. Halle: M. Niemeyer, 1885.

Edition of two shorter Latin versions, L^2 and redaction I and IV; enumerates 22 different mss and gives the particulars of the French, English, Danish, and Slavonic forms of the legend.

543   ———, ed. *Uber die Quellen der mittelenglischen Paulusvision.* Halle: P. unk., 1883.

Not seen.

544   ———. "Über die Quellen der Mittelenglischen Versionen der Paulus-Vision." *Englische Studien* 7(1884):534-65.

Discusses Greek and Latin versions and the Old English mss in an attempt to establish redactions. Presents an edition of the Latin text (redaction IV), pp. 544–47.

545   Dwyer, M.E. "An Unstudied Redaction of the *Visio Pauli.*" *Manuscripta* 32 (1988): 121–38.

Vat. Pal. Lat 220, ff. 56r–60r, called Redaction XI, consisting of extracts from a long Latin version of the *VP* and interpolated material. Provides a transcription and continues the study of redactions of the *VP* developed by Silverstein.

546   Gardiner, see **32**, pp. 13–46.

Includes English translation of the vision with notes and bibliography.

547   Healey, Antonette Di Paolo, ed. *The Old English Vision of St. Paul.* Speculum Anniversary Monographs 2. Cambridge, Mass.: Medieval Academy of America, 1978.

Presents an annotated diplomatic edition of the Old English text of Oxford, Bodleian Junius 85–86 with facing Latin sources and source notes. Introductory material includes discussion of ms (composition, contents, and provenance), the Latin and Old English tradition of the VP, the language of the text, and elements of the Old English vision (body-soul legend, respite of the damned, correspondence of punishment to sin, and influences). Includes notes, glossary, word index, and selective bibliography. Rev. by Theodore Silverstein in *Medium Aevum* 50:120–22.

548   Hennecke, Edgar, and Wilhelm Schneemelcher, eds. *New Testament Apocrypha.* English trans, ed. by R. McL. Wilson. 2 vols. Philadelphia: Westminster Press, 1964, 2:755–98.

English translation of the Latin text (Paris ms) published by James (**552**). Discusses the history of the text, translations, contents, and sources.

549   Horstmann, C. "Die Vision des Heiligen Paulus."
         Englische Studien 1(1877): 293–99.

         Annotated diplomatic edition of Old English text
         based on the Vernon ms, with brief introduction.

550   ———. *Die Vision des Heiligen Paulus, aus M.S. Vernon.*
         Erlangen: P. Unk., 1877.

         Not seen.

551   Hyde, Douglas. *Legends of Saints and Sinners.* London:
         T.F. Unwin [191_], 95–109.

         English translation of Irish vision, which was
         published in original language in Religious Songs of
         Connaught, vol. 2.

552   James, Montague Rhodes. *Apocrypha anecdota.* Texts
         and Studies 2.3. Cambridge: Cambridge University
         Press, 1893, 11–42.

         Annotated edition of Paris ms. Edition of Latin L^1
         version. Includes general introduction on apocrypha and a
         particular introduction of the long Latin version of the *VP*,
         discussing other versions and comparing the long Latin
         version with the the Greek and Syriac texts and the
         abbreviated Latin version edited by Brandes (**543**).

553   ———. *The Apocryphal New Testament.* Oxford:
         Clarendon, 1955, 525–55.

         English translation based on the L^1 text of the Paris
         ms, with readings and passages drawn from the Coptic,
         Greek, and Syriac versions.

554   Jeanroy and Vignaux, see **461**, pp. 121–28.

        Diplomatic edition of Languedoc version found in ms
        Toulouse B.M. 894.

555   Jones, John Morris, and John Rhys. *The* Eludidarium
        and Other Tracts in Welsh. Anecdota Oxonensia.
        Medieval and Modern 6. Oxford: Clarendon, 1894.

        Not seen.

556   Kastner, L. E. "Les versions françaises inédites de la
        descente de Saint Paul en enfer." *Revue des langues
        romanes* 48 (1905): 385–95; 49 (1906): 49–62, 321–
        51, 427–49.

        Presents editions of four French versions of the *VP*:
        the version of Henri d'Acri (pp. 385–95), an anonymous
        version (49–62); the version of Geoffroi de Paris (321–
        51); and a Burgundian version (427–49).

557   ———. "The Vision of Saint Paul by the Anglo-Norman
        Trovère Adam de Ross." *Zeitschrift für franzosische
        Sprache und Literatur* 29 (1905–6): 274–90.

        Discusses mss; presents a critical edition of the
        Anglo-Norman text.

558   Luiselli Fadda, Anna Maria. "Una inedita traduzione
        anglosassone della 'Visio Pauli.'"*Studi Medievali* ser.
        3, 15.1 (1974): 482–95.

        Discusses the text found in Bodleian Junius 85
        (eleventh century), and presents an Old English edition
        with facing Italian translation and critical apparatus.

559   Meyer, P. "La Déscente de Saint Paul en Enfer."
        Romania 6 (1877): 11–16.

        Mentions five rhymed French versions and provides
        a critical edition based on three mss.: Paris B.N. Fr.
        24429, 24432, and 15606.

560   ———. "La Descente de Saint Paul en Enfer, poème
        français composé en Angleterre." *Romania* 24
        (1895): 357–75, 589–91.

        Discusses a Latin ms, not included by Brandes (**543**),
        Paris B.N. 1631, and six rhymed French versions of the
        VP. Provides an annotated edition (pp. 365–75) of
        Toulouse B.M. 815. Briefly introduces the ms and work.
        Includes a reproduction of two illustrated pages.

561   ———. "Légendes Hagiographiques en Français."
        Historie Littéraire de la France. Paris: Imprimerie
        National, 1906, 33:372.

        Lists six French verse versions: three composed in
        England; one by Adam de Ros, one by Gaufroi de Paris,
        and one by Henri d'Arci. Refers to *Notices et extraits* 35,
        155–56, where the mss are enumerated.

562   Morris, Richard. *Old English Miscellany*. Early English
        Text Society 49. London: Trübner, 1872; rpt. New
        York: Greenwood, 1969.

        Annotated diplomatic edition of the Old English *VP*
        based on the Vernon ms.

563   Os, see 53, pp. 264–66.

        Reprint of Meyer, (**560**).

564   Owen, see **54**.

Discussion of French medieval accounts of hell and how in their treatments the authors disclose the general medieval idea of the Christian otherworld. Includes a diplomatic edition of the French text of the Vision of Paul from Dublin, Trinity College 951 Cl. I.5.19.

565   Ozanam, see **55**, pp. 425–37.

Annotated diplomatic edition of French Adam de Ros text of the thirteenth century text.

566   PL 94:501–502.

Latin text of redaction IV from Bede's *Homilies,* Bk. 3.

567   Rutherfurd, Andrew. "The Vision of Paul." *Ante Nicene Fathers* 9. Ed. by Alexander Roberts and James Donaldson. New York: Scribner's, 1917–25, 149–66.

English translation of Latin L^1 version based on James (**552**), with brief introduction.

568   Silverstein, Theodore. *Visio Sancti Pauli: The History of the Apocalypse in Latin together with Nine Texts.* Studies and Documents 4. London and Toronto: Christophers, 1935.

Introduction covers the Western tradition of the *Apocalypse of Paul*: origin, spread, rise of different versions, and influences, focusing on the long Latin texts.

Presents editions of nine versions of Latin texts and redactions. Includes bibliography.

569   Villari, see **72** , *Antiche Leggende,* 77–81. *Annali* 129.

Italian edition based on Florence Cod. Mag. Cl. XXXVIII, 127, compared with Cod. Mag. Palch IV, 56 and Vat. Palatino 73.

570   Williams, J. E. C. "Irish Translations of the *Visio Sancti Pauli.*" Eígse 6 (1948–52): 127–43.

Discusses briefly the development of the VP, Latin versions, its popularity in the Middle Ages, and two Irish translations, which he discusses with slightly greater detail, then presents diplomatic editions of both Irish texts: the Royal Irish Academy 24 P 25 and Liber Flavus Fergusiorum.

Studies

571   Acker, Paul. "The Going-Out of the Soul in the Blickling Homily IV." *English Language Notes* 23 (1986): 1–3.

A brief discussion of the *VP* as the source for the going-out-of-the-soul passage in the Blickling Homily.

572   Ancona, see **3**, pp. 43–48.

Treats the antecedents of Dante in general and gives some particular attention to the Paul, Brendan, Tundale, Patrick, and Alberic visions. He does not make firm connections between these and the *Divine Comedy,* but indicates a general milieu of vision literature, which does not detract from Dante's originality.

573   Bartsch, Karl. *Grundriss zur geschichte der provenzalischen literatur.* Elberfeld: Fridericks, 1872, 57.

         Brief notice on ms: Paris La Vall. 14, B.L. 139.

574   Carey, John. "Visio Sancti Pauli and the Saltair's Hell." *Eigse* 23 (1989): 39–44.

         Discusses the relationship of the *Saltairna Rann* and the *VP* and concludes that the evidence indicates that Canto V drew heavily on a lost redaction of *VP*, probably a hybrid version based on redactions III and IV.

575   Casey, R. "The Apocalypse of Paul." *Journal of Theological Studies* 34 (1933): 1–32.

         Traces the development and transmission of the *Apocalypse of Paul* up to the Middle Ages.

576   Ciluffo, Gilda. "La versione anglosassone della Visio Pauli." *Schede medievali* 4 (1983): 78–83.

         Comparison of two editions of the Anglo-Saxon text.

577   Dumville, see **87**.

         Discusses the relationship between the *Fis Adamnán* and the *VP*.

578   Foster, see **29**, 2:452–53, 645–486.

         Description and bibliography of the English *Vision of St. Paul.*

579   Hasenfratz, Robert. "Eisegan stefne (*Christ and Satan*
       36a), the *Visio Pauli,* and ferrea vox (*Aeneid* 6,
       626)." *Modern Philology* 86 (1989): 398–410.

       The "iron voice" or "tongue" that drives home the
       unspeakable and everlasting torments of hell found in
       Anglo-Saxon homiletic literature probably has its source
       in a Latin redaction of the *VP.*

580   Mertens, Volker. "Die Frühumhd. 'Visio Sancti Pauli.'
       Untersuchungen zur Quellenfrage." In *Wurzburger
       Prosastudien.* Ed. by Peter Kesting. Medium Aevum
       Philologische Studien 31. Munich: Wilhelm Fink,
       1975, 1:77–91.

       Discusses the different versions of the Latin *VP.*

581   Owen, D. D. R. "'The Vision of St. Paul': The French
       and Provençal Versions and Their Sources."
       Romance Philology 12 (1958): 33–51.

       Examines sources and discusses the latitude with
       which authors treated sources and, hence, the difficulty of
       clear cut lines of redactions.

582   Secret, F. "*La Revelación de Sant Pablo.*" *Sefarad* 28
       (1968): 45–67.

       Article on a 1494 printed text of a Spanish translation
       of the *Apocalypse of Paul,* with a listing of the contents,
       the text of the prolog, and the dedication of the "Ensis
       Pauli."

583   Seymour, see **65.**

Discusses a tradition in the literature of dying where the soul is unwilling or unable to leave the body through certain members (mouth, nose, etc.) either because they are sanctified (in the case of the righteous person) or are guarded by devils (in the case of sinners). Mentions two visions of the otherworld in this context, *Vision of St. Paul* and the *Vision of Ezra*.

584 Silverstein, Theodore. "Irish Versions of the *Vision of St. Paul.*" *Journal of Theological Studies* 24 (1922–23): 54–59.

Presents an English translation of the Old Irish *VP* based on the fragmentary text in the *Liber Flavus Fergusiorum* and compares it briefly with the Latin text of the *VP*. Discusses another later and more popular Irish *VP* (**551**), examining elements of the Irish Paul visions and their relationship to other versions of the *VP* as well as to works such as the *Vision of Merlino*. Concludes that other medieval versions of the *VP* were known in Ireland from an early date and that older versions (especially the Latin) were probably also studied in Ireland.

585 ———. "Studies in the Apocalypse of Paul." Diss.: Harvard University, 1930.

Not seen.

586 ———. "Dante and the *Visio Pauli.*" *Modern Language Notes* 47 (1932): 397–99.

Links the pit of the eleventh canto of the *Divine Comedy* to the scene between Paul and the Archangel Michael in the *VP*, claiming that, if it is not merely a coincidence, it indicates evidence of Dante's knowledge of the *VP*.

587 ———. "The Source of a Provençal Version of the *Vision of St. Paul.*" *Speculum* 8 (1933):353–58.

Proposes redaction I or II as basis for the Provencal text rather than redaction IV, as was proposed by Jeanroy and Vignaux (**555**).

588 ———, see **398**.

Discusses the bridge in a Latin redaction of the *Visio Pauli* in relationship to the *Vision of Leofric*. However, he concludes, that the bridge in *Leofric* is clearly dependent on the bridge in the *Dialogues* of Gregory the Great and therefore does not present a reason to suspect an earlier date of composition for this redaction of the *VP*.

589 ———. "Did Dante Know the Vision of Saint Paul?" *(Harvard) Studies and Notes in Philology and Literature* 19 (1937): 231–47.

Examines the question of direct influence of the *VP* on Dante, concluding that a general influence through the broader tradition of vision literature seems likely.

590 ———. "The Vision of Saint Paul: New Links and Patterns in the Western Tradition." *Archives d'Histoire Doctrinale et Littéraire du Moyen Âge* 34 (1959): 199–248.

Reconstruction of the particular form of the Latin ancestor of the main corpus of the western redactions of the *Visio Pauli* and the relation of these redactions to each other.

591 ———. "The Date of the *Apocalypse of Paul.*" *Medieval Studies* 24 (1962): 335–48

Discusses the origin and development of this work from the Greek text of the fifth century to its Syriac, Coptic, and Latin versions, recontact with the Greek text in the twelfth century resulting in new Latin and German versions.

592   ———. *Visiones et revelaciones S. Pauli. Una nuova tradizione di testi latini nel Medio Evo.* Rome: Accademia Nazionale dei Lincei, 1974.

Discusses the problem of determining influences and relationship among versions of the *VP*, the relationship to the *Divine Comedy* and the other vision literature. This is basically a discussion of the state of studies when Silverstein undertook his work on the *VP*. He provides a stemma of the relationship of the texts and establishes a history of the Latin versions and their family from the sixth to the fifteenth century.

593   ———. "The Graz und Zurich Apocalypse of Saint Paul: An Independent Medieval Witness to the Greek." *Medieval Learning and Literature: Essays Presented to Richard William Hunt.* Ed. by J. J. G. Alexander and M. T. Gibson. Oxford: Clarendon, 1976, 166–80.

Discussion of these two texts demonstrating a further medieval access to the ancient Greek text of the apocalypse, independent of the main Latin tradition. These texts also offer additional witness to the nature of the ancient text itself and the variant forms which it took.

594   Stegmüller, Fr. *Repertorium Biblicum Medii Aevi.* Madrid: Consejo Superior de Investigaciones Cientificas, Instituto Francesco Suarez, 1940 (1950), 240–45.

Not seen. According to Silverstein: erroneous summary of Western tradition of *VP*.

595 Tabor, James D. *Things Unutterable: Paul's Ascent to Paradise*. Lanham, Md.: University Press of America, 1986.

A study of Paul's thought and religious experience set in its wider Jewish/Greco-Roman context. Chapter 4 focuses on the ascent described in 2 Corinthians 12:2–4, seeing it as Paul's own particular vision and version of that most general and Hellenistic (and human) hope – escape from mortality. Not really about the *Visio Pauli*, but about the biblical text and its significance in Paul's theology of salvation and apocalypse.

596 Ward, see **306**, 2 (1893): 397–416.

Includes description of Latin mss: Royal 8 E. xvii, Harley 2851, Arundel 52, Add. 26,770, Royal 13 C. vi., Royal 11 B. iii., Royal 11 B. x., Royal 8 F. vi., Royal 8 C. vii.; French mss: Cotton Vesp. A. vii, Add. 15,606; and English ms: Add. 22,283.

597 Wright, Charles D. "Beowulf, Blickling Homily and the *Visio Pauli*." *Old English Newsletter* 22, n.2 (1989): Appendix 29–39.

Abstract of paper in Anglo-Saxon studies conference discussing significant verbal parallels between the *VP* and the *BH* and similar but less conclusive parallels between the *VP* and *Beowulf*, indicating that both have drawn on the *VP*, probably in a vernacular version.

598   ———. "Some Evidence for an Irish Origin of Redaction
           XI of the *Visio Pauli.*" *Manuscripta* 34 (1990): 34–
           44.

           Responding to an article by Dwyer (**545**), this author
           draws attention to evidence for an Insular, probably Irish,
           origin; also corrects a few errors in the Dwyer transcript.

THE VISION OF A POOR WOMAN (VISIO CUIUSDAM PAUPERCULAE MULIERIS)

Latin, early ninth century (after 818), vision of hell. The visionary, simply described as a poor woman, is led through a geographically undistinguished hell by a guide in the habit of a monk, where she sees Bernard, king of Italy and the nephew of Louis the Pious; Picone, a friend of Charlemagne; and Louis's first wife Ermengarde, all suffering purgatorial pains, but apparently expecting release.

The poor woman also sees Louis's name on the wall of the earthly paradise, but it has been defaced, as her guide explains, after the assassination of his nephew, Bernard. She is sent back to warn Louis to repent, but her natural reticence makes it necessary for her guide to warn her three times and finally to blind her, promising to restore her sight when she fulfills her obligation to warn the emperor.

A most interesting aspect of this vision is that the woman is simply a messenger. Her soul is not of concern, only the souls of the mighty.

Before the wall of the earthly paradise when the woman is told to read the names of those listed – those who will gain entry – she complains that she does not know how to read and is offhandedly and miraculously given the gift of literacy. Miraculous literacy is found in other medieval works but is found particularly in works related to women, who often had to rely on the supernatural gift of literacy, since they were generally denied this gift in the natural course of things. (See Petroff, **60**, p. 28).

Sources
599   Ciccarese, see **13**, pp. 394–401.

195

Latin text based on Houben (**600**) with facing Italian translation. Includes brief introduction on the nature of this work as a political vision. Provides some notes to the text.

600   Houben, Hubert. "Visio cuisdam pauperculae mulieris. Uberlieferung und Herkunft eines frühmittelalterlichen Visionstexts (mit Neuedition)." *Zeitschrift für Geschichte des Oberrheins* 124, n.f. 85 (1976): 31–42.

Discusses mss and previous editions, and provides a critical edition of Latin text.

601   Wattenbach, Wilhelm, and Wilhelm Levison, ed. *Visio cuiusdam pauperculae muleris.* Deutschlands Geschichtsquellen im Mittelalter bis zur Mitte des Dreizehnten Jahrhundert. 5 vols. Berlin: P. unk., 1885, 1: 260–61; rpt. by Heinz Lowe in *D G Q M Vorzeit und Karolinger* 3: 317–18 (Weimar, 1957).

Not seen.

THE VISION OF ROTCHARIUS

Merovingian vision of the early ninth century, associated with the church of St. Benedict near Fleury. A monk named Rothcharius, while lying sick, is led by an angel to heaven where he sees the Congregation of the Saints gathered together in a marvelous building. Here he meets Charlemagne, then visits two further buildings: the third of which is a place for the punishment of sinners immersed in fire and rained upon with hot water. Among those in the third house he meets three of his brethren.

Sources
602   Wattenbach, W., ed. *Anzeiger für Kunde der deutschen Vorzeit*, n.f. 22 (1875): 72–74.

Brief introduction, which discusses mss, followed by a diplomatic edition of the Latin text based on the Petersburg manuscript.

THE VISION OF ST. SADALBERGA

Sadalberga (c.605–670), abbess of Laon, is reported, in the ninth century *Vita Sadalberga abbatissae Laudunensis,* to have received a vision of heaven, briefly described, in which she is carried up by a splendid white bird. Heaven is described in terms of a river amd a pleasant meadow full of fragrant flowers where she meets Magobert, Amiliana's son – evidently an acquaintance of hers – and Anseris, bishop of Soissons. He shows her the gates of paradise, the city of God and the seats of the twelve apostles. She is promised a place in heaven, but because her sisters at the abbey need her, she is sent back to life again.

Sources
603   MGH SRM 5:64–66.

     Vita Sadalbergae in annotated critical edition of Latin text by B. Krusch.

604   McNamara, Jo Ann, and John E. Halborg. *Sainted Women of the Dark Ages.* Durham, N.C. and London: Duke University Press, 1992, 192–93.

     English translation from the *Vita,* with brief introduction and notes.

THE VISION OF SALVIUS

This Latin vision of heaven, in about 950 words, is included in Bk. 7, ch. 1 of the *History of the Franks,* by Gregory of Tours, who briefly describes the life of Salvius (d. 10 Sept. 584), a layman, a monk, an abbot, and finally an anchorite. For one night he lies as if dead while he is carried to heaven by two angels. There he enters a gate into an abode with a floor that gleams like gold and silver. He sees a great multitude of spirits "without sex" and hears the voice of God from a luminous cloud. When he returns to life he recounts what he has heard and seen, how he was nourished by heavenly food, but he believed that he should not have told what he saw. Gregory claims that he heard this story from Salvius himself and in anticipation of doubters he quotes Sallust: "when we record the virtue or glory of good men, the reader will readily approve such things as he deems that he himself might do, but such things as are beyond these he holds untrue."

In his *Historia,* Gregory also includes the *Vision of Sunniulf* and the *Visions of Chilperic* (Bk. 7, ch. 4), the latter are not included here, since they are not true visions of heaven and hell but rather political justifications for the assassination in 584 of Chilperic, a king of Neustria, who is seen in hell in visions of both Gregory and by one Guntram.

Sources
605   Buchner, Rudolf, ed. *Gregory of Tours, Historiarum libri decem.* Berlin: Rutten & Loening, 1957, 2:89–95.

Latin edition with facing German translation.

606	Dalton, O. M., trans. *Gregory of Tours, History of the Franks.* 2 vols. Oxford: Clarendon, 1927, 2:285–88.

	English translation based on Omont and Collon edition (**608**). Introduction discusses Gregory, the mss., and earlier printed editions of the *Historia,* and also the history of the Merovingian kingdom, church, and life.

607	MGH SRM 1:1: Bk. 7 ch. 1.

	Latin text edited by B. Krusch and W. Levison.

608	Omont, Henri and Gaston Collon, ed. *Gregoire de Tours, Histoire des Francs, Texte des Manuscrits de Corbie at de Bruxelles.* Collection de textes pour servir à l'étude et à l'enseignement d'histoire. Paris: Picard/ Poupardin, 1913, 252–56.

	Annotated edition of Latin text.

Studies
609	Ciccarese, Maria Pia. "Alle origini della letterature delle visioni: it contributo di Gregorio di Tours." *Studi Storico Religiosi* 5 (1981): 251–66.

	Not seen.

THE VISION OF STEPHANUS DE MARUSIACO'S FATHER

Also called the *Vision of a Reliable Man* (*Probus homo*), this vision, is included in the Etienne de Bourbon's *Tractatus de diversis materiis praedicabilibus* and entitled "De subvensione beatorum," this work was written in Latin before 1261. It describes in a text of about 700 words, the man's visit to a house of torment, to a river full of animals, which is crossed by a bridge. Mary helps him across the bridge, after which he returns to his body bearing a warning.

Sources

610   Lecoy de la Marche, A. *Anecdotes historiques, legendes et apolyges tirés du recuel inédit d'Etienne de Bourbon, dominicain du XIIIe siècle*. Paris: Rounard, 1877.

Not seen.

THE VISION OF SUNNIULF

This very brief Latin vision (about 150 words) is included in *The History of the Franks* (Bk. 4, ch. 33) of Gregory of Tours with the *Vision of Salvius* and the *Visions of Chilperic* (Bk. 7, ch. 4), the latter are not included here, since they are not true visions of heaven and hell but rather political justifications for the assassination in 584 of Chilperic, a king of Neustria, who is seen in hell in visions of both Gregory and by one Guntram.

Sunniulf, abbot of the Monastery of Randau in Puy-de Dôme, once "ruled his flock by entreaty," but he has a vision of a river of flame with people immersed to different parts of their bodies. A narrow bridge crosses the river to a great white house, but many fall from the bridge in attempting to cross it. Sunniulf learns that those who are remiss in strictly governing their flock are doomed to fall. This vision causes him to rule his monks with greater severity. This vision can be dated to c. 563, which is the year that Marius Aventicum *(Chron.)* dates the flood at Taurendunum, which is described by Gregory as occurring at about this same time, but is assigned to 571 by Gregory.

Sources

611   Buchner, see **605**, 1: 40.

Latin edition with facing German translation.

612   Dalton, see **606**, 2:142.

English translation based on Omont and Collon edition (**608**). Introduction discusses Gregory, the mss, and earlier printed editions of the *Historia,* and also the history of the Merovingian kingdom, church, and life.

613   MGH SRM, see **607**, 1:1, Bk. 4 ch. 33.

        Latin text edited by B. Krusch and W. Levison.

614   Omont and Collon, see **608**, 132–33.

        Annotated edition of Latin text.

Studies
615   Ciccarese, see **609**.

        Not seen.

THE VISION OF THURKILL

This lengthy (c. 8500 words) vision of heaven, purgatory and paradise is dated October 1206 (All Souls' Week) by both Ralph of Coggeshall and Roger of Wendover. The former is the redactor who translated Thurkill's account into Latin. The preface mentions the visions of Tundale, the monk Stephen, the Monk of Eynsham, St. Patrick's Purgatory, and Gregory's *Dialogues*. The work recalls in part the *Vision of Gunthelm* and the *Testament of Abraham*.

Thurkill is a humble laborer in Essex, England. He is visited one evening by St. Julian, who takes him on an otherworld journey, leaving his body behind. Thurkill has only been guilty of not tithing correctly — for which his punishment is a whiff of the stench of a certain fire. Unlike many other visions, this vision is not particularly meant to save Thurkill's soul but to make him a witness on earth to the torments and rewards of the otherworld. Some of the devils actually reinforce this point by saying that they don't want Thurkill to see what goes on in their realm, because he will then warn those on earth, and the devils will lose their followers.

The physical structure of the otherworld is particularly interesting in this vision, because heaven is constructed like a huge church and called the Congregation of the Saints where all are assembled after they die to wait for their assignments. During his vision Thurkill also meets St. James and St. Domninus. He sees St. Nicholas, Michael the Archangel, Peter and Paul and a devil riding one of the recently deceased nobles of England like a horse.

On the way to the mount of joy there is a purgatorial fire, a cold and salty lake, and a bridge with thorns and stakes. St. Nicholas presides over purgatory and, as in the *Monk of Eynsham's Vision,* is responsible for helping the souls toward salvation. There seems to be a unique occurrence here, of the use of scales to weigh souls to determine whether they merit reward or punishment. St. Paul and a devil weigh the souls, and each takes charge of those who tip the scale toward their side. The scale is such a popular image in medieval visual representations of the Last Judgment that it is interesting that it does not occur more often in visions.

The place of punishment, quite unusual compared to what we have seen before, is described as a theater. Those to be punished are arranged around on seats, which themselves inflict pain. The devils view a spectacle that involves the sinners re-enacting their sins and then being tortured fiercely by demons before being finally returned to their seats. The sinners who are singled out for punishment include a proud man, a priest who took goods from his people and did not perform his duties, a soldier who killed and robbed, a lawyer who took bribes, adulterers and adulteresses, slanderers, thieves, incendiaries and violators of religious places, and bad merchants. Bloomfield[1] mentions that in Thurkill's Vision "punishments [are] meted out in hell, by class as well as by sin."

Adam appears briefly in this vision as a symbol of the slowly evolving history of salvation.

This vision is also considered to be significantly linked to medieval pilgrimage practices. (See **620.**)

When Thurkill returns to earth he is reluctant to tell the story of his vision until he is warned in another vision that the reason he was given the first vision was so that people would learn from it.

Sources
611   Gardiner, see **32,** 219–36.

         Includes an English translation based on Ward (**616**) of vision with notes and bibliography.

---

1. Bloomfield, Morton. *The Seven Deadly Sins: An Introduction to the History of a Religious Concept with Special Reference to Middle English Literature.* East Lansing, Mich.: Michigan State College Press, 1952, p. 397.

612   Roger of Wendover, see **332**, 3: 190–209.

         Diplomatic edition of Latin text under 1206.

613   ———, see **333**, 2: 221–35.

         English translation based in Coxe edition (**332**).
         Preface discusses Roger, the nature of his work, and his
         sources.

614   ———. *Flores historiarum*. Ed. by H. G. Hewlett. Rolls
         Sers. 84. 4 vols. London: Public Record Office,
         1887, 2:16–35.

         Edition of Latin text under 1206.

615   Schmidt, Paul Gerhard, ed. *Visio Thurkilli relatore, ut
         videtur, Radulpho de Coggeshall*. Leipzig: Teubner,
         1978.

         Latin edition based on B.L. Royal 13 D.v. and
         Cambridge Univ. Library Mm. VI. 4. Includes an
         introduction on the author, sources, the four mss, and the
         text. Also includes bibliography

616   Ward, H. L. D., ed. "The Vision of Thurkill, Probably by
         Ralph of Coggeshall, Printed from a MS. in the
         British Museum." *Journal of the British Archeo-
         logical Association* 31 (1875): 420–59.

         Introduction to the text discusses its relationship to
         other visions. Provides English translation plus lightly
         annotated diplomatic edition of Latin text of Royal 13.
         D.v.

Studies

617   Bigogiari, D. "Were There Theatres in the Twelfth and Thirteenth Centuries." *Romanic Review* 37 (1946): 201–24.

      In response to the Loomis and Cohen article (**622**), he discusses the words relating to "theater" as rhetorical survivals from ancient texts; in the case of Thurkill these words were used in a most imaginative way, and therefore no indication that theaters actually existed during this period.

618   Gurevich, see **367**.

      Discusses the problem of the interrelationship of oral and written traditions, in the *VT* and the *Vision of Gottschalk,* which are in constant and complex interaction.

619   James, M. R., ed. *Catalogus bibliothecae saec. XIV ex. exarartus.* Oxford: P. unk., 1926, nos. 60 and 76.

      Not seen. List of mss formerly in Peterborough Abbey Library.

620   King, Georgiana Goddard. "The Vision of Thurkill and Saint James of Compostela." *Romanic Review* 10 (1919): 38–47.

      Looks at *Thurkill* from the point of view of its connections with other visions, its dream psychology, and the fragments of pilgrim's lore that circulated regarding Compostela and other shrines along the pilgrimage route; suggests that the theater in *Thurkill* has its origins in amphitheaters or bullrings. Article quotes freely from

Ward translation (**616**) commenting on the above topics along the way.

621   Liestøl, see **433**, 96–101.

Synopsis of the *VT* and a discussion of it as a possible source for the Vision of Olav Asteson (*Draumkvaede*).

622   Loomis, R. S., and G. Cohen. "Were There Theaters in the Twelfth and Thirteenth Centuries." *Speculum* 20 (1945): 92–98.

Uses passages regarding "deludis theatralibus" in *Thurkill* as one of nine passages providing evidence of "theaters" in the twelfth century. (See **617**.)

623   Marshall, Mary H. "Theatre in the Middle Ages: Evidence from Dictionaries and Glosses." *Symposium* 4 (1950): 1–39, 366–89.

Using evidence from glossaries and dictionaries, the author concludes that the word "theater" was a very inclusive word, generally referring to an open place for spectacles. Discussion of Thurkill , pp. 377–78.

624   Rockelein, see **62**.

Combines psychological and ethnological approaches in a study of Otloh of Emmeran with particular reference to the "collective" visions of *Gottschalk, Thurkill, Tundale,* and *Owayne (St. Patrick's Purgatory).*

625   Schmidt, P. G. "The Vision of Thurkill." *Journal of the Warburg and Courtauld Institutes* 41 (1978):50–64.

Examination of relationship between the visionary and redactor, and an investigation of the influences to which the visionary's account is subjected before it takes its final form. Concludes that an unknown redactor has "expanded, modified, abridged and enhanced" the visionary's account based on borrowings, although the figure of Thurkill is not invented. Provides information on four mss (p. 57).

626   Ward, see **306**, 2 (1893):506–15.

Description of Latin mss: Royal 13 D. v. and Cotton Julius D. v.

THE VISION OF TUNDALE

Tundale's Vision was written in 1149 by an Irish monk who had travelled to Regensburg in Bavaria. This lengthy vision (10,500 words) was enormously popular in the Middle Ages and was translated into at least thirteen different languages. The story of this vision is also related by Helinand and Vincent of Beauvais. There seems to be an indebtedness to the visions of Sunniulf, Paul, Drythelm, and the Boy William, as well as the *Voyage of St. Brendan.*

Tundale was an Irish knight and was almost surely on the road to hell. Tundale is a true sinner, who is struck dead, but a little warmth on his left side prevents his friends from burying him. In the meantime his soul is met by its own guardian angel who leads Tundale on a tour of hell and heaven.

Tundale, like the Knight Owein, is severely punished as he journeys through a hell that is strictly divided into punishments for particular sins. These are mentioned in sequence, beginning with murder. This description of hell is the most fully and consistently developed one before the "Inferno" of Dante. In hell many of the usual features are present, like pits of fire, mountains of fire and ice, valleys of fire, narrow bridges, furnaces and ovens, a horrible beast who tortures fornicators, the forge of Vulcan and finally the pit of hell. There is also a beast belching flames and consuming the souls of the damned. All the souls tortured in the upper regions of hell, that is, not in the pit of hell, are not yet finally judged, so the greater part of this hell of Tundale actually serves as a place of purgation, although it is not actually called purgatory. Lucifer is given a full and careful description, but the description of the devil suffering is quite unusual. After hell, Tundale then proceeds on a gradually rising path visiting better and still better souls in fields and pavilions, then over walls of precious stones and metals and finally through gates.

Throughout this vision the angel guide and Tundale maintain an important discussion on the nature of divine mercy and justice, a running dialogue that prefigures the one between Dante and Virgil. This replaces the discussion found in many of the other visions of holier men, which generally discuss the need for Masses, prayers, and alms for the dead. Here we are concerned with the salvation of this individual soul, who has come so close to perdition, rather than with the extra things that the living can do for those already dead. There is no mention of the efficacious effects of the good works of the living on the status of the souls of the dead.

As in the *Divine Comedy*, Tundale meets many whom he recognizes. Particularly, as he approaches heaven, he meets some kings and bishops who were known to him in life.

Sources

627   Bellemans, A. T. W., et al. *Tondalus' visioen. Naar het Gentsche handschrift met inleiding, aanteekeningen en bibliographie.* Antwerp: Nederlandsche Boekhandel, 1945.

Not seen. Dutch edition.

628   Castellane. *Ayssi comensa lo libro di Tindal.* N.p. P. unk., 1890.

Not seen. Provençal and French edition.

629   Corazzini, Francesco, ed. *Visione di Tundalo.* Scelta di curiosità litterarie inedite o rare 128. Bologna: Gaetano Romagnoli, 1872.

Contains an edition of the Italian text based on five mss. The brief introduction discusses the narrative; the original Latin text, mss, and editions; other translations from the Latin; and the Italian text and mss.

630   Dahlgren, Fredrik August. *Skrifter till läsning fur Klosterfolk.* Stockholm: Norstedt, 1874–75.

Not seen. Swedish edition.

631   Friedel, V.-H., and Kuno Meyer, ed. *La Vision de Tondale, textes français, anglo-normand et irlandais.* Paris: H. Champion, 1907.

Editions of the French prose versions (London B.L. Add. 9771 and Paris B.N. Fr. 763) and the Anglo-Norman verse fragment (Dublin, Trinity College Cod. membr. vel. in quarto, no. 312) and Irish fragment (Dublin, Trinity College Ms H. 3. 18). The last translated by Muirgheas mac Paidin í Maoilchanaire, c. 1510. Introduction on Tundale, Marcus (the author), the Irish setting and characters, the date, and the connection to Regensburg.

632   Gardiner, Eileen, ed. "An Edition of the Middle English 'Vision of Tundale.'" Ph.D. Diss.: Fordham University, 1980.

A critical edition of the Middle English text based on the five existing manuscripts.

633   ——, see **32**, 149–95.

English translation of Latin vision with notes and bibliography.

634   Giuliari, Giovanni Battista C. *Il Libro di Theodolo, o vero la Visione di Tantalo.* Bologna: Gaetano Romagnoli, 1870.

Edition of an Italian (Veronese) version of Tundale with a description of the fourteenth century ms in the library of Verona, a discussion of the language of the text, and also a brief examination of the relationship of this work to the *Divine Comedy*.

635   Ivsic, Stjepan. "'Tundalovo videnje.' u Lulicevu zborniku." *Jugoslavenska akademija znanosti i umjetnosti* 41 (1948): 119–57.

   Not seen. Text in Croatian and Italian.

636   Jagíc, V. "Zur Visio Tundali." *Archiv für Slavische Philologie* 35 (1914): 501–13.

   Not seen. Edition of Old Croatian fragment.

637   Jeanroy and Vignaux, see **461**, pp. 55–119.

   Provides an edition of the Languedoc text of *VT* found in Toulouse B.M. 894.

638   Kraus, Carl von. *Deutsche Gedichte des zwölften jahrhunderts.* Halle: M. Niemeyer, 1894, 217–46.

   Not seen.

639   Mearns, Rodney, ed. *The Vision of Tundale, edited from B.L. MS Cotton Caligula A II.* Middle English Texts 18. Heidelberg: Carl Winter, 1985.

   An edition of the Middle English text based on the Cotton ms.

640   Palmer, Nigel F., ed. *Visio Tnugdali: The German and Dutch Translations and Their Circulation in the*

Later Middle Ages. Münchener Texte und Untersuchungen der deutschen Literatur des Mittelalters 76. Munich and Zurich: Artemis, 1982.

Discusses mss, the Latin text and its transmission, the German and Dutch translations; provides description of mss and early printed editions; also discusses circulation of vernacular versions. In an appendix lists other German and Dutch otherworld visions.

641   Peters, Emil. *Die Vision des Tnugdalus: Ein Beitrag zur Kulturgeschichte des Mittelalters. Wissenschaftliche Beitrage zum Jahresbericht des Dorotheen städtisches Realgymnasium zu Berlin Ostern.* Berlin: R. Gaertners, 1895.

Introduction discusses the origin and development of the vision legend. Presents modern German translations of the Vision of the Soldier from the Dialogues of Gregory the Great, the Vision of Drythelm, and the Vision of Tundale (rpt. from Wagner, **651**), the latter preceded by an introduction of its own.

642   Picard, Jean-Michel, trans. *The Vision of Tnugdal.* Intro. by Y. de Pontfarcy. Dublin: Four Courts, 1989.

Not seen. English translation, includes bibliography.

643   PL 212:1038–55.

Latin version of *VT* from Helinand of Froidmont's *Chronicon*.

644   Saggio di un volgarizzamento inedito della visione di Tundale. N.p.: P. unk., 1886.

Not seen. Edition of Italian text.

645　Schade, Oscar, ed. *Visio Tnugdali.* Halle: Libreria Orphanotrophei, 1869.

Not seen. Latin edition.

646　Turnbull, W. B. D. D., ed. *The Visions of Tundale: Together with Metrical Moralizations and Other Fragments of Early Poetry.* Edinburgh: Thomas G. Stevenson, 1843, 1–76.

A diplomatic edition of the Middle English text from a ms in the Advocates collection of the National Library of Scotland, Edinburgh. Introduction discusses the Cotton ms in the British Library and various early printed editions.

647　Verdeyen, R. ed. Tondelus' *Visioen: Naar een Brusselschhandschrift uit gegeven.* Van alle tijden 4. Groningen: J. B. Wolters, 1921.

Annotated diplomatic edition of Dutch text with introduction in Dutch.

648　———— and Endepols, see **477**, 2:1–177.

Annotated critical edition of Middle Dutch texts.

649　Villari, see **72**.

Diplomatic edition of Latin text (3–22) based on ms in the Spencer Library and critical edition of Italian text (23–50) based on four editions.

650   Vincent of Beauvais, see **139**, Vol. 4 (*Speculum historiale*): 1127–33.

      Bk. 27, ch. 8–104: Latin version of text entitled *De raptu anime Tundali et eius visione.*

651   Wagner, Albrecht, ed. *Visio Tnugdali lateinisch und altdeutsch.* Erlangen: Andreas Deichert, 1882.

      Not seen. Latin and Old German edition.

652   ———, ed. *Das Mittelenglische Gedicht über die Vision des Tundalus.* Halle: M. Niemeyer, 1893.

      A critical edition of the Middle English text based on four mss, the Edinburgh ms, the Bodley ms, and the two British Library mss, using the Royal ms in the B.L. as the base text.

Studies

653   Ancona, see **3**, 523–59.

      Treats the antecedents of Dante in general and gives some particular attention to the Paul, Brendan, Tundale, Patrick and Alberic visions. He does not make firm connections between these and the *Divine Comedy,* but indicates a general milieu of vision literature, which does not detract from Dante's originality.

654   Boas, see **9**, pp. 154–74.

      Study of "primitivism" which examines the idea of the earthly paradise using several examples but in particular the *Vision of Tundale, St. Patrick's Purgatory,* and *St. Brendan's Voyage.*

655 Carozzi, Claude. "Structure et fonction de la Vision de Tnugdal." *Faire Croire: Modalités de la diffusion e de la réception des messages religieus du xiie au xve siècle.* Collection de l'École Française de Rome 51. Rome: École Francaise de Rome, 1981, 223–34.

Discusses the questions of purgatory and physical punishment in the otherworld with particular reference to contemporary theological works on the same questions.

656 Foster, see **29**, 2:455–56, 648.

Description and bibliography on the Middle English Vision of Tundale.

657 Gardiner, Eileen. "A Solution to the Problem of Dating in the *Vision of Tundale.*" *Medium Aevum,* 51 (1982): 86–90.

Examines the thesis presented by Marshall (**661**) and presents a solution to what Marshall sees as internal contradictory information in the vision regarding its year, 1149. Proposes that the vision occurred within the year from March 25, 1148 to 1149.

658 Garrigues, Marie-Odilon. "L'auteur de la Visi Tnugdali Honorius Augustodunensis?" *Studia Monastica* 29.1 (1987): 19–62.

Examines in detail the possible authorship of Honorius Augustodunensis, finding that the evidence is not conclusive.

659 Kenney, see 90, pp. 741–42.

Brief discussion of the text, list of mss, and a bibliography up to 1929.

660   Kren, Thomas, and Roger S. Wieck. *The Visions of Tondal from the Library of Margaret of York.* Malibu, Ca.: J. Paul Getty Museum, 1990.

Contains essays on the tradition of visionary literature in the Middle Ages, the library of Margaret of York, and on the illuminator and illuminations of this particular manuscript; presents color reproductions of the miniatures along with a translation of parts of the text. Includes a select bibliography.

661   Lawlor, H. J. "The Biblical Text in Tundal's Vision." *Proceedings of the Royal Irish Academy* 36.c.19 (1924): 351–74.

Biblical texts were available in Ireland in two versions: an Old Latin text and the Vulgate. Based on a comparison of the VT with these two biblical versions, there is evidence that Marcus used the Old Latin text of the gospels, Apocalypse, probably Acts, and the Epistles, except for the Pauline Epistles, which were mainly O.L. with a mixture of Vulgate. His psalter was of the Vulgate with a mixture of O.L.

662   Marshall, J. C. Douglas. "Three Problems in the 'Vision of Tundale.'" *Medium Aevum* 44 (1975): 14–22.

Discusses the discrepancy between the date given by the author for the vision and the events attributed to that date, and dates it alternatively four or more years after 1149. Claims that the apparent inconsistencies in the presentation of Tundale result because this is the first vision of a sinner, and the author falls back on traditional treatments of the visionary in heaven, making Tundale seem better than he was originally described. Claims that the reason for the scarcity of Celtic influences in what is supposedly an Irish work is because the author is freely innovating with a more complex tale.

663   Meneses, Paolo. "Le recit hagiographique expression doctrinaire de la spiritualite medievale." *Diogene* 139 (1987): 53–72.

Not seen.

664   Mussafia, Adolfo. *Sulla Visione di Tundalo.* Vienna: C. Gerold, 1871.

Discusses the author and composition of the *Vision of Tundale* and the abbreviated versions (e.g. in Vincent of Beauvais' Speculum historiale); compares the opening chapters in various versions to establish the earliest versions; discusses the German, Dutch, English, Swedish, Icelandic, Spanish, Provencal, French, and Italian versions – often providing mss and/or editions. Discusses two Italian versions in particular. Appendix provides an edition of the Latin text of the *Visio Ezra,* which occurs in a ms from Heiligenkreuz with a *Visio Tundalo* and a *Visio Wettini.* The point of this small book (52 pages) is to examine the relationship among different versions, especially since Mussafia considers this the most important vision of heaven and hell except for the *Divine Comedy.*

665   Ovidio, see **103**.

In the context of Dante's "Purgatorio" Ovidio discusses the non-eternal nature of punishment in the *VT*; also discusses the *Vision of Alberic* in this context.

666   Rockelein, see **62**.

        Combines psychological and ethnological approach in
        a study of Otloh of Emmeran with particular reference to
        the "collective" visions of Gottschalk, Thurkill, Tundale,
        and Owein *(St. Patrick's Purgatory).*

667   Seymour, St. John Drelincourt. "Studies in The Vision of
        Tundal." *Proceedings of the Royal Irish Academy*
        37.c.4 (1926): 87–106.

        Discusses how this vision casts an important light on
        the development of diocesan episcopacy between the
        Synods of Rathbreasail and Kells, and discusses Marcus
        as a supporter of the reforms in the Irish church. It also
        presents a developed form of the newer eschatological
        views (especially in connection with the purgatorial
        doctrine), which came into Ireland as part of the reform
        movement of the first half of the twelfth century.
        "Possibly it was written with the object of making these
        views popular." Seymour identifies many historical
        places and characters in the *VT*. He also devotes attention
        to dating, placing the vision in 1148 and the composition
        in 1149. The *VT* represents views on eschatology more in
        line with western Christendom then previously in Ireland.
        Discusses biblical versions (see Lawlor above), liturgical
        elements, sources (Virgil, Rule of St. Benedict, Gregory's
        Dialogues, and the visions of Drythelm, the Monk of
        Wenlock, the Boy William, Adamnán, Alberic and
        Wetti).

668   ——, see **69**.

        An account of the views held by the early Irish
        church on the otherworld and particularly on the
        development of the purgatorial doctrine. Discusses both

imrama and visions (Furseus, Laisrén Adamnán, and Tundale; plus the non-Irish Drythelm and Monk of Wenlock). Covers heaven, hell, division of souls, fire of doom, and purgatory. He argues that before the ninth century the Irish church conceived of hell as a place from which souls could be released through the intervention of a saint or the pious deeds of the living. From the tenth century purgatory becomes separate from hell and the later Irish visions describe a separate purgatorial state – reflecting a view more in line with orthodoxy and probably related to the revolution in ecclesiastical matters taking place in Ireland before the close of the twelfth century.

669   Spilling, Herrad. *Die Visio Tnugdali: Eigenart und Stellung in der mittelalterlichen Visionsliteratur bis zum Ende des 12 Jahrhunderts.* Munchener Beitrage zue Mediavistik und Renaissance Forschung 21. Munich: Arbeo-Gesellschaft, 1975.

Examines the *VT* as a work reflecting a particular medieval spirit; discusses the author and development of the work; the topography and the structure of its otherworld, its ethical foundation, its literary merit, concluding with an overall analysis of the place of vision literature in the Middle Ages. Two excursuses discuss the metamorphosis of Lucifer and the tradition of *St. Patrick's Purgatory.*

670   Verdeyen, R. "La Date de la *Vision de Tondale.*" *Revue Celtique* 28 (1907): 111–12.

Concludes that the discrepancies between the date, 1149, and the events described are the result of confusion between recent events and the date of the transcription.

671   Wagner, Albrecht. *Ausgabe der Visio Tnugdali.* Erlangen: P. unk., 1882.

Not seen.

672   Ward, see **306**, 2 (1893): 416–35, 746–47.

Includes descriptions of Latin mss: Harley 3776, Cotton Tiberius E. i., Add. 27,424; French ms: Add. 9771; English mss: Cotton Caligula A. ii., Royal 17 B. xliii.; Latin mss: Harley 4987, and Add. 11,437.

A REVELATION OF PURGATORY BY AN UNKNOWN FIFTEENTH-CENTURY WOMAN

Middle English, 1422, Winchester, England; visionary and author unnamed.

The unknown woman addresses this revelation of her vision to her confessor. It is actually a series of four visions, the first of which occurs on St. Lawrence Day, 1422. The other three occur on the three following nights, as the woman witnesses and helps the soul of one, Margaret, through the three fires of purgatory; and as she explains she reveals her vision of the three great fires of purgatory to profit the souls of the living. The initial vision is of the punishment of religious men and women who failed to lead an exemplary life. At first the woman is without a guide, but the second vision focuses on Margaret who subsequently acts as the woman's guide explaining many aspects of purgatory and punishment. Margaret also hopes the woman will be a source of her salvation, and she beseeches the woman for help in freeing herself from the purgatorial fires. She details a long list of prayers and masses to be said for her by specific individuals.

On the third night the woman witnesses the suffering of Margaret in the first fire as the devil explains her sins and sufferings. Other punishments of both religious and lay persons are revealed, and Margaret explains these sins and punishments. On the fourth night Margaret passes through the second and third purgatorial fires and explains how purgatory is structured.

Although this vision lacks clear geographical descriptions, the descriptions of physical tortures more than compensate since they are gruesome and vivid in detail. An interesting feature is the little fiery cat and dog who follow Margaret about tearing at her body. This vision is also significant in its complex structure, being four related visions, in its preservation of a particular aspect of woman's visions, in that it is personal and confessional, and yet it

223

uses many of the more conventional otherworld elements found in the more popular literary visions.

Sources
672   Harley, Marta Powell, ed. "A Revelation of Purgatory: A Critical Edition Based on Longleat MS 29." Ph.D. Diss.: Columbia University, 1981.

        Not seen.

673   ———. *A Revelation of Purgatory by an Unknown Fifteenth Century Woman.* Lewiston, N.Y.: Mellen Press, 1985.

        Introduction on the doctrine of purgatory; the Christian afterlife in popular visions; and the "revelation" and the woman visionary. Provides a critical text based on three mss (Longleat 29, Lincoln Cathedral 91 (Thornton), and Oxford, Bodleian Eng. th.c.58); and translation into modern English.

674   Horstmann, C., ed. *Yorkshire Writers.* London: Swan Sonnenschein, 1895, 83–92.

        Lightly annotated diplomatic edition of Middle English text from the Thornton ms.

Studies
675   Foster, see **29**, 2:456–57, 648–49.

        Description and bibliography on the Middle English *Revelation of Purgatory.*

676   Harley, Marta Powell. "The Origin of a Revelation of Purgatory." *Reading Medieval Studies* 12 (1986): 87–91.

Identifies various individuals who appear in this work, helping to establish the date and milieu of the author and visionary.

THE VISION OF WALKELIN (WALCHELIN)

Walkelin, a priest of Bonneval in the diocese of Liseux, has a vision of purgatory one night when returning home after administering to a sick man. His vision, described in about 2200 words, is included in an entry for the beginning of January 1091, at the time of the siege of Courci, in Odericus Vitalis' *Ecclesiastical History* (Bk. 8, ch. 17), a twelfth-century, Latin work on the Normans.

Walkelin attempts to hide behind some meddlar trees to escape the notice of a troop passing by. This troop turns out to be a procession of the dead who suffer purgatory. This vision is interesting in that purgatory is not located elsewhere or in an otherworld, but in our own world. Walkelin sees many who are known to him, but these come especially from the ranks of the knights who are tortured for their various sins. The priest has a confrontation with these souls when he attempts to steal one of their horses to use as a proof of his vision. Instead he returns with a facial scar as proof. Walkelin is not very cooperative with the requests of the souls until he meets his brother, and although he continues to resist, he is finally convinced to undertake some attempt to relieve the suffering of those in purgatory through prayer and alms. and he amends his own life, which is marred by some small vices.

This vision is interesting in the various similarities it has with the descriptions of the Witches' Sabbaths described in Carlo Ginzburg's *Ecstasies* (New York: Penguin, 1992). For instance: the early January date, the parade of souls, the souls riding animals.

Sources

677   Chibnall, Marjorie, ed. and trans. *The Ecclesiastical History of Odericus Vitalis.* Oxford: Clarendon, 1973, 4:236–50.

Presents Latin edition and English translation. Vol. 1 includes an introduction to the *Eccles. Hist.,* which discusses other editions and the mss (pp. 115–23).

678   Forester, Thomas. Th*e Ecclesiastical History of Ordericus Vitalis.* 4 vols. London: Bohn's Antiquarian Library, 1853–65., 2:511–20.

Annotated English translation based on Le Prévost edition (Paris, 1838–55). Includes English translation of M. Guizot's introduction to an earlier French translation, which covers, with a true nineteenth-century perspective on the "dark" ages, the life of Odericus, the purpose and method ("unimaginative") of his composition, and the mss.

THE VISION OF WETTI (VISIO WETTINI)

This Latin vision dates from 824. It was written in prose (length: c. 3500 words) by Heito (*exabbate Augiensi et Basiliensi exepiscopo*) in the same year and then re-composed in verse (length: c. 7000 words) by Walafrid Strabo in 837. This is the first account of a vision in verse. It was influenced by the Vision of Paul, the Apocalypse, and possibly the Vision of Barontus. It mentions the *Dialogues* of Gregory and its redactor may have known the visions of a Poor Woman and Rothcarius. Wetti is referred to in the *Vision of Bernoldus*.

Wetti, a monk in the monastery at Reichenau, falls ill on October 30, 824. He tells his vision on November 3 and dies the following day, November 4.

During a first brief vision Wetti speaks with an angel. When this vision ends he asks his brothers to read to him from the Dialogues of Gregory the Great. After the reading he rests himself, and as he lies, as if dead, his soul is led by the angel on a tour of the otherworld. On this journey he sees many who are known to him.

This vision is particularly interested in the sins of the clergy and in sins of a sexual nature. Wetti claims that while the angel, his guide, mentions most sins once, "again and again the angel introduced a discussion of the sin of sodomy...five times and more [he said] that it should be avoided." At one point, right after mentioning "sodomy" he mentions "the plague," – a unique connection in this genre.

A particularly interesting point of this vision is the author's efforts at verifying its truth by mentioning facts that would not have been known to Wetti but were revealed to him in his vision and then confirmed independently – a device later used to excellent dramatic effect by Dante.

The vision particularly calls the rich and the powerful to task for abusing their power by amassing great fortunes through extortion and plunder.

This vision strongly encourages aiding the souls of the dead with Masses, prayers, and alms, as the duty of the clergy and other Christians.

Wetti spends a considerable time while in the areas of the blessed seeking intercessors among the virgins, martyrs, and saints to help him on his course toward heaven. He is apparently accused of giving bad example to his followers, and although not physically punished, he does undergo some psychological punishment as he tries to gain assurance that he will be able to obtain forgiveness.

His obligation after his vision is to have it copied down and disseminated so that others can learn from what he has seen. Apparently there have been other cases when a monk has been shown some of these very same things, but the visions and their messages fell into oblivion and only a few remembered them. Most important apparently is Wetti's message for the reform of religious houses for both men and women in Gaul and western Germany. Such elements point to this vision's ties with the Lotharingian monastic reform movement connected with St. Benedict of Aniane in the early ninth century and with Louis the Pious at Aachen.

Sources

679   Ciccarese, see **13**, pp. 406–445.

        Heito's Latin text based on MGH (**682**) with facing Italian translation. Includes brief introduction (pp. 402–5) on the nature of this work with regard to the others in the collection. Provides some notes to the text.

680   Gardiner, see **32**, 65–79.

English translation of vision with notes and bibliography.

681   MGH PLAC. 2:267–75.

Heito's text ed. by E. Dümmler.

682   MGH Poetae M.E. 2:259–334.

Introduction on Walafrid Strabo and his poetry; including discussion of mss, followed by a critical edition of Heito's Latin prose version (268–75); and critical edition of Strabo's Latin verse version (301–34). Ed. by Ernst Dümmler.

683   PL 105:771–80.

Edition of Latin text of Heito's version based on Mabillion, *Act. ord. S. Bened.*, saec. iv, parte 1.

684   PL 114:1065–82.

Edition of Latin text of Strabo's version.

685   Traill, David A. *Walahfrid Strabo's Visio Wettini: Text, Translation and Commentary.* Bern and Frankfurt/M: Lang, 1974.

English translation and Latin edition of Strabo's text with commentary and bibliography. Revision of dissertation (Univ. California, Berkeley, 1971), which originally included a critical apparatus and Heito's prose version. This book includes indices and a "Note on the Latin Text." Introduction includes studies of the life of Walafrid, circumstances leading to his composition of the

VW, the place of the *VW* in the history of vision literature, mss (7), editions, and meter.

Studies
686   Kleinschmidt, Erich. "Zur Reichenauer Uberlieferung der 'Visio Wettini' im 9. Jahrhundert." *Deutsches Archiv zur Erforschung des Mittelalters* 30 (1974): 199–207.

Discusses ms tradition.

687   Plath, Konrad. "Zur Entstehungeschichte der Visio Wettini des Walahfrid." *Neues Archiv der Gesellschaft für altere deutsche Geschichtskunde* 17 (1892): 261–79.

Not seen.

THE VISION A WOMAN (QUIDAM MONACHO CUIDAM DE VISIONE FEMINAE CUISDAM REFERT)

Fragmentary Latin vision from shortly after 757 recorded in a letter from Lull, bishop of Mentz. In approximately 700 words this letter records a vision of hell with sinners immersed in a river of fire and tormented on a wheel, plus a vision of the earthly paradise and three heavens.

Sources
688   MGH, Epistolae 3 (Merowingingici et Karolini aevi 1): 403–5.

Latin text ed. by E. Dümmler.

INDEX

Aachen 229
Aafjes, Bertus 56
abuse of power 229
Acker, Paul 187
Adam 118, 205
Adam de Ros 179, 184, 185, 186
Adam, St. Hugh's biographer 141
Adam, subprior of the monastery of Eynsham 137
Adeliza, queen of Henry I, 67
adulterers and adulteresses 205
Aeneus 45; see also Virgil, *Aeneid*
Aherne, Consuelo Maria 42, 45, 48, 132
Alberic of Settefrati 31, 33
Aldericus 149
Alexander VI, pope 152
Alexander, Paul J. 1
All Souls' Week 204
allegory 1, 16, 17; relationship to vision literature 5
Allen, Philip S. 121
amanuensis 11
Amat, Jacqueline 1
Ancona, Alessandro D' 1, 32, 68, 165, 187, 216
angels as guides 101, 104, 197, 211; Emmanuel and

Hélos 31; see also Raphael, St. Michael
Anglo-Irish visionary 146
Anglo-Saxon visions 2
Annales regni Francorum 99
Annals of Saint-Bertin (*Annales Bertiniani*) 99
Ansellus of Rheims 35
Anti-Christ 101
Antin, Paul 112
Apocalypse of Elias 179
Apocalypse of Enoch 15
Apocalypse of Esdrae 6, 101–03; see also *Vision of Ezra*
Apocalypse of Mary xviii, 10
Apocalypse of Paul, see *Vision of St. Paul*
Apocalypse of Peter, see *Vision of St. Peter*
Apocalypse of Sedrach 101–03; see also *Vision of Ezra*
Apocalypse of Zephaniah 179
Apocalypse xxx, 4, 50, 228
apocalypses, medieval 1
apocalyptic literature 27; visions xviii, xx, xviii
apocrypha in Ireland, eastern and western 19
apocryphal literature xix, 33, 76, 103
Apollonius von Tyrlant 84

gates, twelve 180
Gatto, G. 9
Gaufroi de Paris 160, 184, 185
Gautier de Metz 57, 58
Geck, Elisabeth 56
gems and precious stones xxx
geographical space 4
Gerard 31
Gerould, G. H. 128
Gerritsen, W. P. 76
Gignani, Antonietta 56
Giles, J. A. 92, 96, 97, 106,
   136
Ginzburg, Carlo, *Ecstacies*,
   xxxii, xxxiii, 226
Giraldus Cambrensis 175;
   Topographia 178
Giuliari, Giovanni Battista C.
   212
Gjallar Bridge 146
Glauber, Raoul, *Historiarum
   libri cinque* 26, 36
godmother as Mother of God.
   146
goldsmith 137
Good Friday 137, see also
   Easter
Gospel of Nicodemus 35
Grat, Felix 99
Gregory of Tours, *History of
   the Franks* 5, 199, 202
Gregory the Great, see St.
   Gregory the Great
Gregory VII, pope 107
Greven, Joseph 109
Grion, Giusto 158

Grosjean, Paul 124
Gualdo 38
guardian angel 23, 179, see
   also angels and guides
Guerico, Luigi 33
Guibert of Nogent, *De vita sua*
   115; the devil in his works
   116
guides: angels 108, 143; devils
   35; Frannoaldo 43; Michael
   the Archangel 180
Guido, a priest of the Abbey of
   Monte Cassino 31
Guizot, M. 227
Gunther, the hermit 149
Gurevich, A. 10, 110, 207

H. of Sawtry (Saltry) 153,
   159, 160, 164, 167, 175
Haemgisl, *relatio* of 95
hagiography xix, xxiii, 82
Hamburg 38
Hamel, A. G. van 56
Hammer, Wilhelm 76
Hammerich, L. L. 158, 170
hammers xxviii
Hanning, Robert W. 76
Hariulf, *Chronicon Centulense*
   90, 91, 92
Harley, Marta Powell 224
Hasenfratz, Robert 189
Haupt, Richard 39, 40
Healey, Antonette Di Paolo
   182

For Product Safety Concerns and Information please contact our EU
representative GPSR@taylorandfrancis.com
Taylor & Francis Verlag GmbH, Kaufingerstraße 24, 80331 München, Germany